HOW TO CHOOSE WHAT TO
WATCH USING COLOUR

BY WILL TURNER BRETT

The Movie Wheel: How to Choose What to Watch Using Colour

The information provided by The Movie Wheel is for general information
purposes only. All information is provided in good faith, however we make no
representation or warranty of any kind, express or implied, regarding the accuracy,
validity, reliability, availability, or completeness of any information in the book.

Although the publisher and the author have made every effort to ensure that the
information in this book was correct at press time and while this publication is
designed to provide accurate information in regard to the subject matter covered,
the publisher and the author assume no responsibility for errors, inaccuracies,
omissions, or any other inconsistencies herein and hereby disclaim any liability to
any party for any loss, damage, or disruption caused by errors or omissions, whether
such errors or omissions result from negligence, accident, or any other cause.

Inspired by George Brett and Jack Widgery.

In loving memory of
Claire Widgery.

Contents

Page 1 — Introduction

Page 4 — Beware the Algorithm

Page 6 — The Movie Wheel

Page 7 — Emotional Key

Page 8 — The Primary Colours

Page 12 — The Secondary Colours

Page 16 — The Tertiary Colours

Page 22 — Opposite Partnerships

Page 24 — The Wheel in Motion

Page 28 — Finding Purpose

Page 30 — The Elements

Page 34 — Denouement

Page 35-188 — Colour Coded
Film Directory

Page 189 — Acknowledgements

Page 191 — Filmography

Introduction

The first thing to clarify is that this book does not concern colour in the literal sense. Instead, we will use colour as a metaphor to explore how genres blend and create unique works of art.

While this book focuses on genres of film, this conceptual understanding also applies to any other creative discipline. For example, music uses genre to elicit emotion from the listener; cooking uses genre in the form of flavour palettes, represented visually in *The Flavour Thesaurus* (Segnit, Bloomsbury Publishing, 2010); even our personalities tend towards distinctly recognisable collections of elements which could be considered genres.

Indeed, the ways in which we do anything may be considered in terms of genre and visually represented in the most basic form as a spectrum. With this in mind, for the purpose of my explanation, I encourage you to embrace the colourful world of cinema.

If I do not happen to include your favourite flick, do not be dismayed. Instead, be comforted in the knowledge that what I am presenting is a concept – a new dimensionality to understanding movies – which should be converted by the reader into their own personal voice and applied to whatever activity they enjoy the most.

You may ask why colour is the perfect metaphor for genre, and the answer is closely linked with emotion; precise combinations of genres, like colour, can produce fantastically unique tones of human emotion, while on the other hand, if one were to recklessly use all at once, the result would be a bland sludge.

There are common elements between the genres, as well as clear opposites. However, as with colour, the idea is not to see these as hard and fast categories, rather to envision them as a spectrum. The emotional range of each genre blends into the next. While online streaming sites categorise them as simply "Action" or "Romance," etc., movies are necessarily a unique configuration of various genre elements, worthy of more than a simple binary distinction.

My paternal grandfather was an expert colourist – he used pencils to colour publications before colour printing became the norm. He would point out that, although it may seem counter-intuitive to add green to the skin tone of a human subject or red to an oceanic palette, a great artist understands that, in reality, colours do not exist in separation from one another; rather, they exist in harmony. Although we do not always consider it, this is essential to our understanding of the world. The world is one thing. We can break it down into countries or creeds if we choose – still, whichever elements we distinguish must necessarily combine in a particular way to form one whole 'world.' In this way, colour comprises more than meets the eye; it represents a spectral output, the precise balance of which forms the various shapes that we interpret as part of a singular reality.

So, this book will apply that conceptual understanding which concerns the colours we see to the emotions we feel when watching a movie. To put it straightforwardly, a filmmaker might include seemingly contrasting elements in a movie in order to shift the emotional range of the film towards a particular result. For example, had the story of *Titanic* (1997) not taken place in a confined setting – a ship which we all know is doomed (thus providing elements of horror) – then the emotions we would feel as a result of the romance would be diminished.

This book will examine how films balance elements of different genres to create their own unique emotional palettes. In order to do this, we will assign the primary emotions of cinema to the primary colours. We will also define the genres and their opposites. This will enable us to see how different genres work together to elicit emotions.

And why, you might wonder, should we do this? What is the purpose of this understanding? Because it affords us greater freedom when it comes to how we select a movie, which is becoming more and more necessary.

Beware the Algorithm

Despite our desire for freedom, in reality, choice has nowadays become its own challenge. The evermore mountainous range of content seems daunting when approached without guidance. As a result, *the algorithm* often serves as our path into the vast unknown; the path inevitably becomes well-trodden, and so perhaps we test adjoining paths. However, the problem with sticking to pathways is that we are unable to discover new areas.

Although the various online streaming sites each use their own algorithmic calculations, they adhere to a similar formula, and user data is shared. As a result, we tend to refer to them all collectively with a definite article in the manner of a leader: *the* tour guide; *the* president; *the* algorithm. Our previous choices are aggregated in order to generate similar suggestions based on, among other things, the primary genres of movies. However, what this fails to acknowledge is that we — all of us — have infinite emotional capacity and that many people want movies to help *expand* their emotional capacity, rather than limit it. Instead, we find in practice that, when the mood strikes for something off the beaten track, the algorithm becomes a severe hindrance. (The importance of variation will be discussed in more detail in a later chapter.)

Moreover, one might fairly argue that viewing figures resulting from algorithm-influenced audiences do not truly reflect their ever-changing demands; as our ability to make a free choice is impeded, our decisions become less representative of who we are. As such, a false impression is created regarding what audiences want to see more of. Indeed, the algorithm may at least partly be to blame for the large-scale box-office failures of recent years. (Naming no names.)

That is not to say that it is without merit. We are creatures of habit, after all. Nonetheless, *we are also creatures of whim.* To deny this would be to deny our own childlike urge to explore the unknown, albeit from the comfort of a couch. With that said, even the most intrepid explorers need basic tools, and understanding the emotional effects of genre serves as a high-beam torch into the darkness.

Most of us know how we feel, or how we would like to feel, at least better than we know the details of film theory. So, *The Movie Wheel* translates movies into emotions using a simple visual for the purpose of helping you make a choice based on how you're feeling right now instead of how you may have been feeling yesterday or the day before.

First, we will assign each genre to a colour so that we can easily see how they work together to elicit different emotions. Sound good? Lets get started.

The Movie Wheel

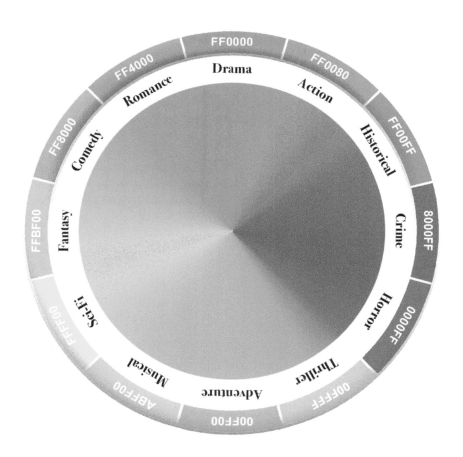

Emotional-Key

	☺ ☹	**Joy-Sadness**
	👍	Catharsis
	🌐	Curiosity
	😌	Disapproval
	🤔 😲	**Intrigue-Fear**
	💣	Suspense
	😬	Courage
	😍	Admiration
	😵 😯	**Awe-Wonder**
	😵‍💫	Inspiration
	💡	Surprise
	😍	Love

The Primary Colours

I have assigned the primary colours – red, blue, and yellow – to the primary cinematic genres, which I propose are respectively drama, horror, and sci-fi.

These genres have been prominent since the dawn of cinema; drama has provided a basis for theatre since long before the days of Shakespeare, while the very earliest films also include works of horror and sci-fi. For example, Georges Méliès produced *The House of the Devil* (1896) and *A Trip to the Moon* (1902), early examples of pioneering works of cinema within the genres of horror and sci-fi respectively. These genres correspond to the fundamental emotional ranges elicited by movies: joy-sadness, intrigue-fear, and awe-wonder.

To put it simply, drama is assigned to the colour red, horror to the colour blue, and sci-fi to yellow. For reasons I will explain, drama makes us feel emotions ranging from joy to sadness, horror makes us feel emotions ranging from intrigue to fear, and sci-fi makes us feel emotions ranging from awe to wonder. Each genre is distinct, yet they all exist in fluid combination, and films use different levels of each in order to fine-tune their emotional impact on the audience.

I should also add that this is how *I* have chosen to lay it out. You might argue that the primary emotions of cinema are different from the ones I proposed, or you might relate different emotions with different genres from the ones I chose. Nonetheless, what I would ask you to acknowledge is the conceptual theory itself – balancing genre is akin to balancing colour, and the levels may be carefully adjusted in order to elicit a particular emotional range.

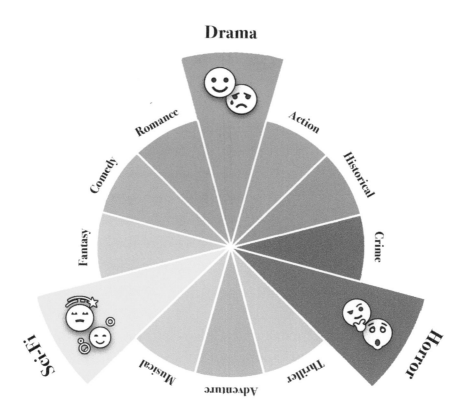

Drama: Joy-Sadness ∎

Joy and sadness are the most fundamental emotions elicited by theatrical performance, as symbolised by the iconic dual masks of Thalia and Melpomene, representing comedy and tragedy respectively. Since ancient times, drama has been crafted in an effort to make audiences feel joy and/or sadness — to cry or laugh.

I have assigned the colour red to this genre, meaning that, according to the colour code outlined in this book, *warmer* colours suggest higher levels of joy and/or sadness.

Horror: Intrigue-Fear ∎

Intrigue and fear work in co-operation with one another. Intrigue draws us in, while fear makes us recoil. This push/pull dynamic is fundamental to the horror genre. Audiences cannot be scared unless their interest is piqued. The more that our attention is captured by something, the more that we will be shocked and terrified when it turns out to be truly horrific – the more captivating the preceding silence, the more terrifying the storm. As Hitchcock said, "There is no terror in the bang, only in the anticipation of it."

I have assigned the colour blue to the genre of

horror. This means that, according to the colour code outlined in this book, *cooler* colours suggest higher levels of intrigue and/or fear.

Sci-Fi: Awe-Wonder

Although awe and wonder may seem similar, they are distinct from one another. In the context of film, I shall define wonder as a fascination with the limitless possibility of that which humanity cannot know. On the other hand, awe means a sense of dread due to such limitless possibility. Therefore, wonder and awe reflect, respectively, a sense of humanity's significance and insignificance within the vastness of that which we cannot know. (Of course, the obvious area we cannot know is outer space; however, this also includes our own imagination, which is equally vast.)

I have assigned the colour yellow to the genre of sci-fi, meaning that, according to the colour code outlined in this book, *brighter* colours (with higher levels of yellow) suggest higher levels of awe and/or wonder.

The Secondary Colours

I have assigned the secondary colours – orange, violet, and green – to the cinematic genres of comedy, historical, and adventure respectively.

These exist in opposition to the primary genres for reasons which I will outline in this chapter.

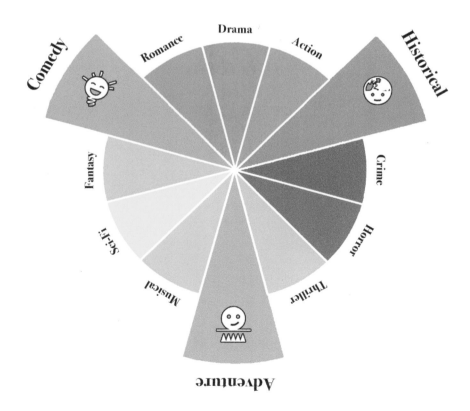

Comedy - Surprise ▪

They say laughter is the best medicine, but against what exactly? Perhaps anxiety. Laughter results from something which shocks us without any real threat. In this way, it is opposite to horror. While horror presents a threat to what we hold dear, comedy tends to reaffirm it.

We may laugh at a tragic situation because we are safe in the shared understanding of the joke – it does not threaten our ideals so much as it surprises us with the hypothetical notion of something different that we recognise as ridiculous and promptly guffaw at.

For example, *Super Troopers* (2001) presents police misconduct as a joke; emphasis is placed on exaggeration so that the audience feels relaxed enough to laugh. The result is a wacky comedy.

On the other hand, *Detroit* (2017) presents police misconduct in a horrific light due to, among other things, its confined setting. Therefore, it threatens our ideals by suggesting that we have serious societal problems which are altogether real. The result is a terrifying crime thriller with a strong sense of horror.

This may seem obvious, but I simply wish to demonstrate how the genres of comedy and horror are theoretically opposed.

Historical - Curiosity ▪

Some would argue that fact and fiction cannot overlap, and that non-fiction, by its very definition, must be devoid of imaginary embellishment. However, *if fact and fiction were to overlap*, then the historical genre would be the main area of contact, as it comprises fictionalisations of true events.

It is opposite to sci-fi, which concerns hypothetical and futuristic worlds. Conversely, historical films present a real world and are set at a particular past time in human history.

Adventure - Courage ▪

This genre encourages us to take on the world. It usually comprises an obviously monumental journey, which places it in opposition to the genre of drama.

While drama concerns internal conflict, adventure concerns external conflict. The adventure genre features huge fire-breathing dragons, while the genre of drama features inner dragons which must be defeated so the character can stop breathing fire, as it were. In this sense, while the drama genre presents a task with little to no instruction, the adventure genre tends to present a massively daunting task and say, "Go on, you can do it!"

That is not to say that either is more or less of a

challenge for the protagonist. After all, which is harder to climb — the mountain you can see or the mountain you cannot? The answer is, of course, neither necessarily; each would present a very different climbing experience, reflecting the opposition of adventure and drama.

The Tertiary Colours

I have assigned the tertiary colours to the following genres, which are opposed to one another:

- Romance - Love
- Action - Catharsis $\longleftrightarrow$
- Crime - Disapproval

- Thriller - Thrill
- Musical - Admiration
- Fantasy - Inspiration

Romance Vs. Thriller

While the romance genre generates tension between two individuals, the thriller genre does the same to create an entirely contrasting emotional effect. In romance, there is the possibility of something good – love – whereas, in the thriller genre, there is the possibility of something bad – sometimes death – but usually, and more precisely, something uniquely crucial, e.g., a student disappointing their teacher, as in *Whiplash* (2014).

Tension is created as these possibilities are presented as uncertain, keeping us gripped for the outcome. Therefore, these genres are opposite in how they use tension to elicit emotion; while romance uses it to elicit love and heartache, the thriller genre uses it to elicit suspense and its eponymous thrills.

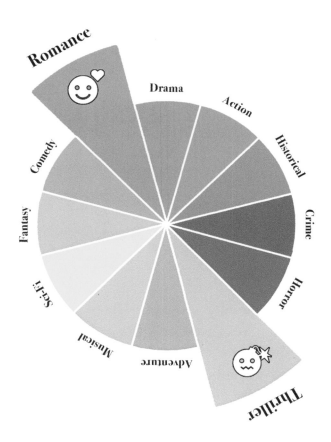

Action Vs. Musical

While the action genre focuses on physical destruction, the musical genre focuses on verbal creation. Technically speaking, these genres might be considered the most exciting due to their visceral nature and prioritisation of spectacle.

The genre of action involves physical matter in all its density, while the musical genre prioritises the non-physical senses, that is to say, words and melody.

That is not to say that sound is inconsequential in action films, nor that musicals do not include physicality, for example, in the form of dancing. On the contrary, this overlap is important to note, since it demonstrates how neither of these genres — nor any — can exist in a state of purity. (This will be discussed in more detail later on.)

Nonetheless, generally speaking, the musical genre says, "Look what we can create with words and melody," while the action genre says, "Look what we can destroy with this massive bomb!" In this way, the musical genre invites us to admire creation, while, contrastingly, the action genre invites us to feel cathartic satisfaction from the spectacle of physical matter being obliterated.

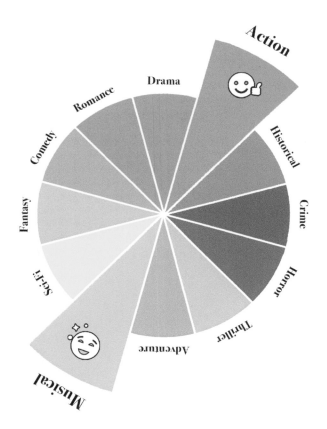

Crime Vs. Fantasy

The crime genre relies on institutional legality, which is commonly understood to be a fundamental reality of human life. Conversely, fantasy relies on no such reality and may not even involve humans.

It should go without saying that legality and morality are not the same; legality is specific to a particular setting, whereas the concept of right and wrong could be described as timeless and non-specific in its application. In this sense, the genres of crime and fantasy are diametrically opposed.

To put it simply, the crime genre invites us to feel intrigue and dismay towards what we know to be *real*, while the fantasy genre invites us to feel inspiration and wonder at what we know to be *unreal*.

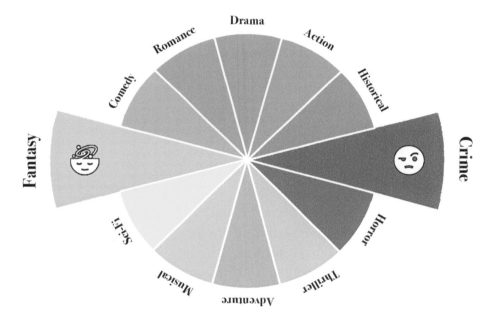

Drama

Romance

Comedy

Fantasy

Action

Historical

Crime

Horror

Thriller

Adventure

Musical

Sci-Fi

Opposite Partnerships

In the world of colour, opposites generally go well together, whilst combining certain other colours results in clashing. Similarly, in cooking, at least based on the visualisation presented in *The Flavour Thesaurus*, opposite flavours compliment each other, whilst certain other flavours impede each other.

However, in the realm of genre and, more specifically, cinema, the rules are less steadfast due to the temporal nature of the medium; it is possible for a film's genre to transition throughout the course of its runtime, which would not be possible with a non-temporal medium. For instance, one would not bake a pie that had one half containing blueberry and the other half steak and ale. This is because the halves would inevitably mix in the moment of consumption to create a confusing blend of palettes. However, with film, that moment of consumption is spread over several hours, so the palette may include a lot of variation, reflecting full freedom of flavour.

Films are able to lead audiences on an emotionally varied journey and cause them to feel different emotions one after the other, even contrasting ones. Audiences enjoy feeling opposing emotions in tandem. So, opposite film genres tend to go well together. With that said, there are exceptions to this, as not all opposite-genre partnerships work well, and the inclusion of other genres is also necessary to maintain the audience's emotional engagement.

Notable examples of successful opposite-genre partnerships include comedy and horror, e.g., *Ghostbusters* (1984), which uses action as a binding agent, as well as romance. Also proven to be highly compatible are romance and thriller, e.g., *Vertigo* (1958), which also involves crime and horror. Drama and adventure work together, e.g., *Easy Rider* (1969), which also involves crime and comedy. Even historical and sci-fi can work, e.g., *Apollo 13* (1995), which also features elements of adventure and drama.

However, the genres of action and crime are not commonly combined with their respective opposites: musical and fantasy. Although some musicals contain elements of action, e.g., the motor-race in *Grease* (1978), there are no obvious examples of films which employ both of these as their main genres. Similarly, while some films employ elements of both the crime and fantasy genres, e.g., *Holes* (2003), there are no clear examples of films which are a genuine crossover of the two.

Therefore, it is fair to summise that opposite-genre partnerships work well in cinema, providing that there are auxiliary genres in the mix too; however, this excludes the genres of action, musical, crime, and fantasy, which, as yet, are not commonly combined with their counterparts.

The Wheel in Motion

Although we may identify the elements of each genre in theory, in practice, none can exist in isolation; I hereby challenge anybody to find a movie which does not include elements of multiple genres.

Movies *must* use different genre elements in order to have an emotional impact, which, after all, is the whole aim of the game – audiences connect with characters on an emotional level, and empathy is crucial.

The reason why it is necessary to mix genres in order to elicit emotion reflects the transience of emotion itself. As the word suggests, *emotion* is always in motion. The word derives from ancient Latin, meaning "to move from." This suggests that it is ever-changing by its very nature. To take this to its logical conclusion, one can summise that, were an emotion not to change, then it would cease to exist entirely: sadness cannot exist except in comparison to joy. Therefore, it makes sense to consider movies in terms of *emotional range*.

The combination of different genres elicits multiple emotions, which is necessary in order to elicit any at all; hypothetically speaking, if a film attempted to elicit but one emotion in isolation, then the result would be no emotion whatsoever. (Consequently, there are no examples of this.)

Even the most genre-defining movies contain elements of genres other than that which they theoretically define. For example, *2001: A Space Odyssey* (1968) is often lauded as a movie that defines the genre of sci-fi, and for good reason. However, were it not for the monumental quest embarked upon by the brave protagonist (providing elements of adventure), its confined setting (horror), or the psychological suspense (thriller) between the astronauts and the A.I. software, then the all-important sci-fi elements — space travel, artificial intelligence, time travel, etc. — would have no emotional impact and thus no cause to exist on the big screen in the first place. Similarly, and by way of further example, *The Exorcist* (1973) is commonly regarded as definitive of the horror genre. However, one would be remiss to ignore the necessity of the mother-daughter relationship (drama) and the experimental technology (sci-fi) used by scientists trying to figure out the mystery (thriller) in creating an emotional impact on the audience.

To take it to the modern extreme, *John Wick* (2014) –possibly the most action of action films — admits that action can only work with the inclusion of non-action elements. Even something as simple as avenging a pet is necessary in order to engage the audience, demonstrating the necessity of genre variation in a tongue-in-cheek way.

So, how does interweaving different genres affect our emotional response? The answer can be neatly illustrated by almost anything involving the senses: for example, a smell may only become noticeable when one moves between that and another smell, or we may tune in more to the music when a new song comes on. With that said, I shall use a gastronomic analogy: the cheese-and-wine party.

Many self-assured sophisticates choose to consume cheese alongside wine. This opposite-flavour partnership is popular because tasting contrasting flavours consecutively allows one to better appreciate each. After tasting wine, the flavour of the cheese seems more potent, and vice versa. In the same way, incorporating elements of different movie genres in combination accentuates each one individually, and, thus, the overall emotional impact of the movie becomes greater than the sum of its parts.

To stick with the analogy for a moment, if one were to only ever consume cheese, wine, or anything else, then the taste would inevitably lose not only its relish but also its potency. One's taste buds would register the flavour less and less. Without wishing to enter a philosophical quagmire, this could be considered as equivalent to the flavour itself ceasing to exist.

In the same way that a repeated physical action may cause numbness, or a continuous sound may cause tinnitus, a movie which does not change our emotional state causes us to feel nothing at all. Therefore, considering how genres mix together is important for both audiences and writers alike when it comes to understanding what emotions a particular movie will summon within us and how.

To take it a step further, if we choose to follow the same habits repeatedly, then we experience a kind of *emotional numbness*. (NB: Therein lie the dangers of the algorithm.) For this reason, it is vital to explore different emotional states in order not to become devoid of emotion entirely —this is where cinema holds the power to do real good in the world; movies can make us feel emotions which we never knew were possible and thereby enhance every other emotion we experience.

To conclude, I pose the following questions. What would the emotional impact of romance aboard *The Titanic* be without the horrific doom of the wreckage? What would audiences feel regarding the historical significance of *Schindler's List* were it not for the dramatic dilemma of a socially conscious protagonist?

Nothing, I tell you.

Nothing at all.

That's why, instead, these movies expertly incorporate a mix of different genre elements in order to elicit the emotions they intend from the audience.

Finding Purpose

As developments in artificial intelligence threaten the jobs of many people in creative and administrative industries, I am squarely reminded of my paternal grandfather.

Over the course of his life, he perfected the craft of colourisation. He used pencils to colour and re-colour all manner of commercial products, ranging from stamps to magazines. Then, in the early 1980s, the proliferation of a new kind of scanner rendered his profession unnecessary – the skill of an individual was no longer required in order to add colour to printed works. No doubt, he asked himself, "What, now, is the purpose of my understanding?" And, no doubt, the answer was obvious to him – colour is omnipresent; understanding its relationship with sight enables us to understand our other senses and even, hopefully as I have made clear, to better understand the relationship between emotion and genre.

Regardless of whether or not the latest technological advancement happens to threaten one individually, one can only benefit from finding the purpose of one's own individual understanding, which provides the best defence against redundancy. As a species, we are unique in unique ways, and uniqueness itself reflects a spectral output akin to colour.

With this in mind, understanding how our own taste is configured prevents us from becoming mere servants of the algorithm; if we understand better the elements of what comprises our choices, then our choices become more free.

The Elements

Each genre comprises various elements, which is how we can predict the emotional effects of their different combinations. These include but are not limited to:

Comedy #FF8000

Elements:

Exaggeration / Absurdity / Wackiness / Parody / Satire / Farce / Personality clash / Wittiness / Slapstick

Romance #FF4000

Elements:

Love interest / Breakup / Wedding / Sex / Romantic tension

Drama #FF0000
(includes family, sports & social issue)

Elements:

Moral dilemma / Friendship / Family / Society / Teamwork

Action
(includes war & kung fu)

`#FF0080`

Elements:

> Violence / Fight sequence / Martial arts / Shooting / Physical destruction / Car chase

Historical
(includes biopics)

`#FF00FF`

Elements:

> Real people / True events / Period setting / Politics

Crime
(includes gangster, prison, heist, & cop dramas)

`#8000FF`

Elements:

> Gangsters / Police / Drugs / Legality / Prison

Horror
(includes slasher, snuff, disaster & creature features)

`#0000FF`

Elements:

> Monster / Zombies / Ghost / Possession / Cult / Confined setting / Brutal killing / Torture / Gore / Impending doom

Thriller
(includes mystery)

`#00FFFF`

Elements:

Suspense / Psychological suspense / Mystery / Personal enemy / Identity switch / Espionage / Evading authority

Adventure
(includes Western, wilderness, & road movies)

`#00FF00`

Elements:

Quest / Traveling / Treasure hunt / Swashbuckling / Inconquerable terrain / Extreme setting

Musical

`#ABFF00`

Elements:

Performance / Song / Dance / Musician

Sci-Fi
(includes cyberpunk & dystopian)

`#FFFF00`

Elements:

Space travel / Time travel / Extra terrestrial / Experimental technology / Artificial intelligence / Futuristic world

Fantasy

(includes animation)

Elements:

Surrealism / Imaginary world / Strange creatures / Myth / Magic / Fairytale

Denouement

My maternal grandfather was a colour consultant for Dulux and, amongst other things, an expert painter. His watercolour paintings would include a *wash* – a light layer of colour to provide an underlying palette for the entire piece. In the same way, the application of genre provides the emotional palette of a film. One of my only memories of him involved him speaking with great passion about the colour wheel and doing his best to impress upon a four-year-old that colours do, in fact, have opposites. How earnest he was, and how grateful I am for the early lesson in mixology from a true master of his craft.

Conceptually speaking, genre works in the exact same way as colour; the only difference is that colour concerns what we see with our eyes, while genre concerns what we feel with our innermost soul. It is certainly worthy of further analysis – cinema can make us feel a much more detailed array of emotions than I have mentioned – nonetheless, this may serve as a brief and introductory guide.

So without further ado, let us look at some examples of films with their own unique emotional palettes, calculated by their balance of different genres.

Colour Coded Film Directory

Disclaimer

This is not a comprehensive list. The movies I include are intended to provide an array of genre combinations, rather than reflect any personal preference.

The movies are ordered by hue, and each colour code signifies an *emotional range*. This does not necessarily mean that similar colours elicit the exact same emotions. However, a similar colour does suggest a similar overall balance of joy/sadness, intrigue/fear, and awe/wonder.

So, if you fancy a scary movie but are unsatisfied with the limited selection of purely horror movies suggested by streaming platforms, simply flick to the cooler-colour section and pick from a range of films which are not restricted by category!

NB; Each 6-digit colour code is preceeded by a hashtag (#) and denotes the specific colour printed on the swatch.

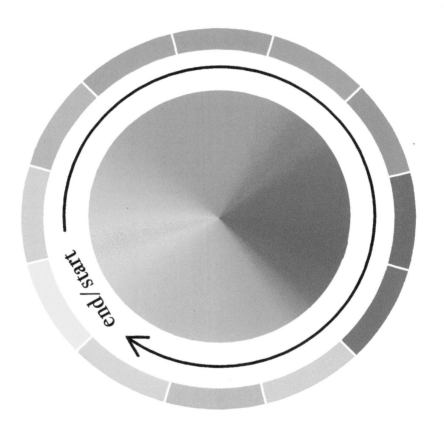

end/start

"We've rebuilt the planet…"

"*The Hitchhiker's Guide to the Galaxy*" (2005)

Written by Douglas Adams & Karey Kirkpatrick
Directed by Garth Jennings

Starring Martin Freeman, Yasiin Bey, & Sam Rockwell

Touchstone Pictures, Spyglass Entertainment, Everyman Pictures

When the Earth is destroyed, a homebody embarks on a voyage to the end of the universe.

Elements:
Space travel / Absurdity / Inconquerable terrain / Surrealism / Friendship

Sci-Fi	5
Comedy	4
Adventure	3
Fantasy	2
Drama	1

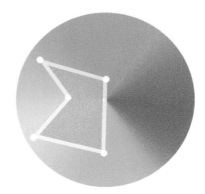

"Well, a little rain
never hurt anybody."

"*Jumanji*" (1995)

Written by Jonathan Hensleigh, Greg Taylor, & Jim Strain
Directed by Joe Johnston

Starring Robin Williams, Kirsten Dunst, & Bonnie Hunt

TriStar Pictures, Interscope Communications, Teitler Film

When two kids play a magical board-game, they unleash the power of the jungle on their house.

Elements:
Magic / Treasure hunt / Absurdity / Family / Love interest / Personal enemy / Confined setting

	Fantasy	5
	Adventure	4
	Comedy	4
	Drama	3
	Romance	1
	Thriller	1
	Horror	1

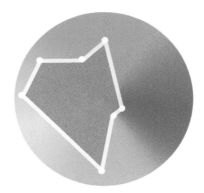

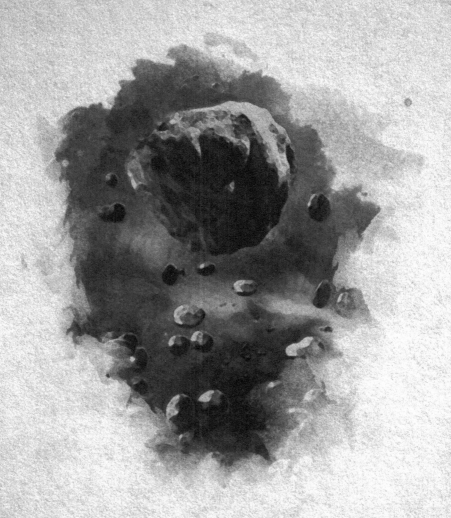

"Don't ever tell me
the odds."

"Star Wars: Episode 5 - The Empire Strikes Back" (1980)

Written by Leigh Brackett, Lawrence Kasdan, & George Lucas | Directed by Irvin Kershner

Starring Mark Hamill, Harrison Ford, & Carrie Fisher

Lucasfilm

Luke Skywalker undergoes jedi training with Yoda, while the forces of evil close in.

Elements:
Space travel / Quest / Shooting / Moral dilemma / Strange creatures / Personality clash

Sci-Fi	5
Adventure	4
Action	4
Drama	2
Fantasy	2
Comedy	1

"At dawn...
Look to the east."

"*The Lord of the Rings: The Two Towers*" (2002)

Written by J.R.R. Tolkien, Fran Walsh, & Philippa Boyens
Directed by Peter Jackson

Starring Elijah Wood, Ian McKellen, & Viggo Mortensen

New Line Cinema, WingNut Films, The Saul Zaentz Company

As the hobbits approach Mordor, their allies battle the evil wizard Saruman's armies.

Elements:
Strange creatures / Quest / Fight sequence / Friendship / Suspense / Personality clash

	Fantasy	5
	Adventure	4
	Action	4
	Drama	2
	Thriller	2
	Comedy	1

"You're definitely one of
the more interesting ones."

"*Everything Everywhere All At Once*" (2022)

Written by Daniel Kwan & Daniel Scheinert
Directed by Daniel Kwan & Daniel Scheinert

Starring Michelle Yeoh, Stephanie Hsu, & Ke Huy Quan

A24, IAC Films, AGBO

A middle-aged immigrant embarks on a multi-dimensional mission to save existance.

Elements:
Experimental technology / Quest / Surrealism / Fight sequence / Family / Absurdity

Sci-Fi	5
Adventure	4
Fantasy	4
Action	3
Drama	3
Comedy	2

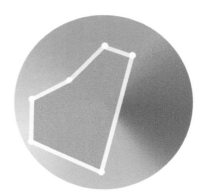

"You can't win against fools."

"*Princess Mononoke*" (1997)

Written by Hayao Miyazaki & Neil Gaiman
Directed by Hayao Miyazaki

Starring Yôji Matsuda, Yuriko Ishida, & Yûko Tanaka

DENTSU Music and Entertainment, Nibrariki, Nippon Television Network

A young outcast on a mission discovers a war between humans and the spirits of the forest.

Elements:
Strange creatures / Inconquerable terrain / Fight sequence / Society / Love interest

■	Fantasy	5
■	Adventure	4
■	Action	3
■	Drama	2
■	Romance	1

  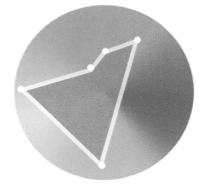

"I believe there's a hero
in all of us."

"*Spider-Man 2*" (2004)

Written by Stan Lee, Steve Ditko, & Alfred Gough
Directed by Sam Raimi

Starring Tobey Maguire, Kirsten Dunst, & Alfred Molina

Columbia Pictures, Marvel Enterprises, Laura Ziskin Productions

The beloved superhero tries to manage his personal life while battling a deranged scientist.

Elements:
Fight sequence / Extreme setting / Advanced technology / Wittiness / Love interest / Family

■	Action	5
■	Adventure	4
■	Sci-Fi	3
■	Comedy	3
■	Romance	2
■	Drama	1

"Love is a many
splendored thing."

"Moulin Rouge!" (2001)

Written by Baz Luhrmann & Craig Pearce
Directed by Baz Luhrmann

Starring Nicole Kidman, Ewan McGregor, & John Leguizamo

Twentieth Century Fox, Bazmark Films

A poor poet falls for a glamorous courtesan, who is also desired by a jealous Duke.

Elements:
Performance / Love interest / Moral dilemma / Surrealism / Wackiness

	Musical	5
	Romance	4
	Drama	3
	Fantasy	3
	Comedy	2

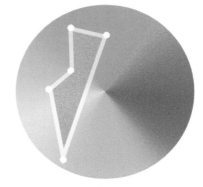

"You might've seen a
house fly. Maybe even
a superfly..."

"Shrek" (2001)

Written by William Steig, Ted Elliott, & Terry Rossio
Directed by Andrew Adamson & Vicky Jenson

Starring Mike Myers, Eddie Murphy, & Cameron Diaz

DreamWorks Animation, Dreamworks Pictures, Pacific Data Images

A grumpy ogre embarks on a quest to rescue a princess in order to reclaim his home.

Elements:
Fairytale / Parody / Quest / Friendship / Love interest / Fight sequence

Fantasy	5
Comedy	4
Adventure	4
Drama	3
Romance	3
Action	3

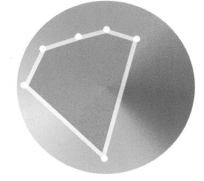

"Yeah, he was pretty old."

"*Dumb and Dumber*" (1994)

Written by Peter Farrelly, Bennett Yellin, & Bobby Farrelly
Directed by Peter Farrelly & Bobby Farrelly

Starring Jim Carrey, Jeff Daniels, & Lauren Holly

New Line Cinema, Motion Picture Association of America

Two dim-witted pals travel across the country to return a briefcase containing ransom money.

Elements:
Wackiness / Traveling / Friendship / Love interest / Gangsters

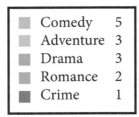

Comedy	5
Adventure	3
Drama	3
Romance	2
Crime	1

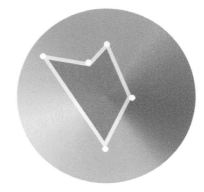

"The past is just a story
we tell ourselves."

#FF8A00

"Her" (2013)

Written by Spike Jonze
Directed by Spike Jonze

Starring Joaquin Phoenix, Amy Adams, & Scarlett Johansson

Annapurna Pictures, Stage 6 Films

In the near future, a lonesome writer develops feelings for an A.I. program.

Elements:
Artificial intelligence / Love interest / Society / Irony

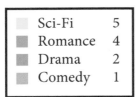

Sci-Fi	5
Romance	4
Drama	2
Comedy	1

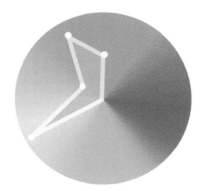

"But which god
should I believe?"

"*PK*" (2014)

Written by Rajkumar Hirani & Abhijat Joshi
Directed by Rajkumar Hirani

Starring Aamir Khan, Anushka Sharma, & Sanjay Dutt

Rajkumar Hirani Films, Vinod Chopra Productions

When an alien is stranded on Earth, his innocence makes people question their own religious beliefs.

Elements:
Satire / Society / Love interest / Performance / Extra terrestrial / Surrealism

	Comedy	5
	Drama	4
	Romance	3
	Musical	2
	Sci-Fi	2
	Fantasy	1

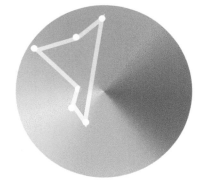

"It's because you're beautiful
inside and out."

"Little Miss Sunshine" (2006)

Written by Michael Ardnt
Directed by Jonathan Dayton & Valerie Faris

Starring Steve Carell, Toni Collette, & Greg Kinnear

Searchlight Pictures, Big Beach Films, Bona Fide Productions

A family travels across the country in a campervan to take their young daughter to a beauty pageant.

Elements:
Family / Personality clash / Quest / Drugs

■	Drama	5
■	Comedy	4
■	Adventure	3
■	Crime	1

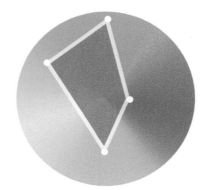

"You ran away from the table."

"*Force Majeure*" (2014)

Written by Ruben Östlund
Directed by Ruben Östlund

Starring Johannes Kuhnke, Lisa Loven Kongsli, & Clara Wettergren

Plattform Produktion, Film i Väst, Rhône-Alpes Cinéma

An unexpected avalanche causes a father to question his place within the family.

Elements:
Family / Irony / Romantic tension / Inconquerable terrain

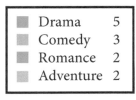

Drama	5
Comedy	3
Romance	2
Adventure	2

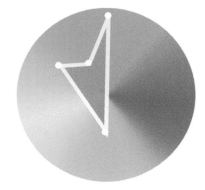

"I wish I knew how
to quit you."

"Brokeback Mountain" (2005)

Written by Annie Proulx, Larry McMurtry, & Diana Ossana
Directed by Ang Lee

Starring Jake Gyllenhaal, Heath Ledger, & Michelle Williams

Focus Features, River Road Entertainment, Alberta Film Entertainment

An intimate sexual relationship between two shepherds is threatened by their respective marriages.

Elements:
Love interest / Society / Inconquerable terrain / Violence

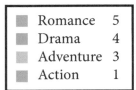

Romance	5
Drama	4
Adventure	3
Action	1

"It's better to help people
than a garden gnome."

"*Amélie*" (2001)

Written by Guillaume Laurant & Jean-Pierre Jeunet
Directed by Jean-Pierre Jeunet

Starring Audrey Tautou, Mathieu Kassovitz, & Rufus

Clauddie Ossard Productions, *Union Générale Cinématographique, Victoires Productions*

A young waitress decides to help others find happiness which sparks her own romantic journey.

Elements:
Love interest / Absurdity / Family / Surrealism / Mystery

Romance	5
Comedy	4
Drama	3
Fantasy	2
Thriller	1

"I'm not going to go on
with a big speech, so I'll
just say this…"

"Bridesmaids" (2011)

Written by Kristen Wiig & Annie Mumolo
Directed by Paul Feig

Starring Kristen Wiig, Maya Rudolph, & Rose Byrne

Universal Pictures, Relativity Media, Apatow Productions

The maid of honour's immense effort to prove her friendship almost ruins the entire wedding.

Elements:
Personality clash / Wedding / Friendship / Police / Traveling

▨	Comedy	5
▨	Romance	4
▨	Drama	3
▨	Crime	1
▨	Adventure	1

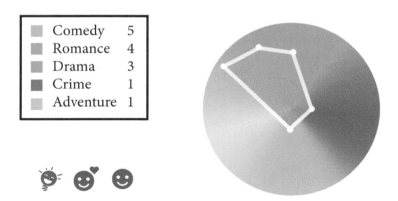

"Why did you let me
eat such a good bowl of
BBQ pork and rice?!"

"*God of Cookery*" (1996)

Written by Stephen Chow, Man-Sang Lo, & Kan-Cheung Tsang | Directed by Stephen Chow & Lik-Chi Lee

Starring Stephen Chow, Karen Mok, & Vincent Kok

Star Overseas

An arrogant chef who stages publicity stunts learns from a street vendor how to defeat his rival.

Elements:
Exagerration / Martial arts / Friendship / Traveling / Love interest / Performance

Comedy	5
Action	4
Drama	3
Adventure	2
Romance	1
Musical	1

"I'm a very good driver."

"Rain Man" (1988)

Written by Barry Levinson & Ron Bass
Directed by Barry Levinson

Starring Dustin Hoffman, Tom Cruise, & Valeria Golino

United Artists, The Guber-Peters Company, Star Partners II Ltd

A selfish salesman learns that he has an autistic brother and attempts to gain his inheritance.

Elements:
Family / Traveling / Legality / Evading authority / Personality clash

Drama	5
Adventure	2
Crime	1
Thriller	1
Comedy	1

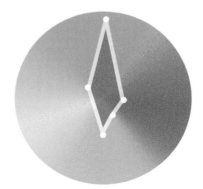

"You would've fought
very bravely and died
very quickly."

"*The Mask of Zorro*" (1998)

Written by Johnston McCulley, Ted Elliott, & Terry Rossio
Directed by Martin Campbell

Starring Antonio Banderas, Anthony Hopkins, & Catherine Zeta-Jones

TriStar Pictures, Amblin Entertainment, David Foster Productions

A young outlaw set on revenge is trained by the legendary Zorro to continue his legacy.

Elements:
Swashbuckling / Fight sequence / Slapstick / Love interest / Society / Period setting

Adventure	5
Action	4
Comedy	3
Romance	2
Drama	2
Historical	2

"Young blood, let me give you a tip... Use your white voice."

"Sorry to Bother You" (2018)

Written by Boots Riley
Directed by Boots Riley

Starring LaKeith Stanfield, Tessa Thompson, & Jermaine Fowler

Cinereach, MACRO, MNM Creative

A young telemarketer's newfound success drives a wedge between him and his friends.

Elements:
Absurdity / Society / Surrealism / Breakup / Monster

■	Comedy	5
■	Drama	4
■	Fantasy	2
■	Romance	2
■	Horror	1

"Hang on a minute. We're supposed to haggle."

"*Monty Python's Life of Brian*" (1979)

Written by Graham Chapman, John Cleese, & Terry Gilliam
Directed by Terry Jones

Starring Graham Chapman, John Cleese, & Michael Palin

HandMade Films, Python (Monty) Pictures

Satirical portrayal of a mistaken messiah in Biblical times, by the world-famous comedy troop.

Elements:
Satire / Period setting / Love interest / Space travel
/ Performance

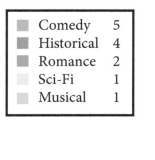

▦	Comedy	5
▦	Historical	4
▦	Romance	2
▦	Sci-Fi	1
▦	Musical	1

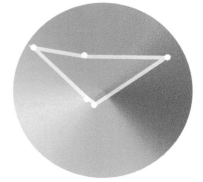

"My heart is stone, and
it still trembles."

"*Les Misérables*" (2012)

Written by William Nicholson, Alain Boublil, & Claude-Michel Schönberg | Directed by Tom Hooper

Starring Hugh Jackman, Russell Crowe, & Anne Hathaway

Universal Pictures, Working Title Films, Cameron Mackintosh Ltd

A fugitive in hiding agrees to help a worker's daughter and struggles to conceal his secret.

Elements:
Performance / Period setting / Love interest / Society / Identity switch / Police

Musical	5
Historical	4
Romance	4
Drama	4
Thriller	2
Crime	2

"The best love is the kind
that awakens the soul..."

"*The Notebook*" (2004)

Written by Jeremy Leven, Jan Sardi, & Nicholas Sparks
Directed by Nick Cassavetes

Starring Rachel McAdams, Ryan Gosling, & Gena Rowlands

New Line Cinema, Gran Via Productions, Avery Pix

When a working-class young man and a rich girl fall in love, class differences promise to get in the way.

Elements:
Love interest / Society / Period setting /
Psychological suspense

■	Romance	5
■	Drama	4
■	Historical	2
■	Thriller	1

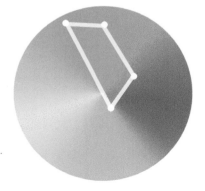

"It's not because we wear skirts. It's because we wear glasses."

"Hidden Figures" (2016)

Written by Allison Schroeder, Theodore Melfi, & Margot Lee Shetterly | Directed by Theodore Melphi

Starring Taraji P. Henson, Octavia Spencer, & Janelle Monáe

Fox 2000 Pictures, Chernin Entertainment, Levantine Films

A team of female African-Americans assist NASA in the United States space program.

Elements:
Period setting / Society / Personality clash / Love interest / Space travel

■	Historical	5
■	Drama	4
■	Comedy	3
■	Romance	2
☐	Sci-Fi	1

"Teaching is a meaningful job."

"Little Big Master" (2015)

Written by Hannah Chang & Adrian Kwan
Directed by Adrian Kwan

Starring Miriam Chin Wah Yeung, Louis Koo, & Winnie Yuen-Ying Ho

One Cool Film Production, Sil-Metropole Organisation, Sirius Pictures
Pictures International

True story about the struggles of the lowest-paid
headmistress in Hong Kong history.

Elements:
Society / Real people / Imaginary world /
Personality clash

■	Drama	5
■	Historical	4
■	Fantasy	2
■	Comedy	1

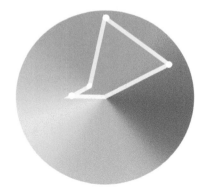

"There lived a princess,
who dreamed of the
human world."

"Pan's Labyrinth" (2015)

Written by Guillermo Del Toro
Directed by Guillermo Del Toro

Starring Ivana Baquero, Ariadna Gil, & Sergi López

Tequila Gang, Estudios Picasso, Esperanto Filmoj

The daughter of a sadistic army officer escapes to a magical yet spooky world.

Elements:
Imaginary world / Period setting / Family / Personal enemy / Monster

 Fantasy	5
Historical	4
Drama	3
Thriller	2
Horror	1

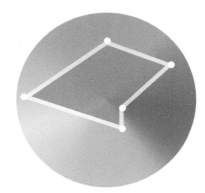

"Where's all the high rollers?"

"Cool Hand Luke" (1967)

Written by Donn Pearce, Frank Pierson, & Hal Dresner
Directed by Stuart Rosenberg

Starring Paul Newman, George Kennedy, & Strother Martin

Jalem Productions

A laid-back drifter is incarcerated in a southern prison and refuses to bend to conformity.

Elements:
Society / Prison / Personality clash / Performance

■	Drama	5
■	Crime	4
■	Comedy	2
■	Musical	1

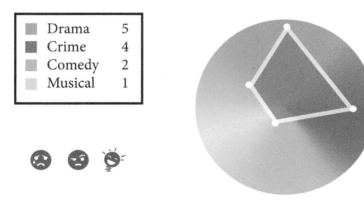

"Don't ever make trouble here.
I'll beat you up each time."

"*Rumble in the Bronx*" (1995)

Written by Edward Tang & Fibe Ma
Directed by Stanley Tong

Starring Jackie Chan, Anita Mui, & Françoise Yip

Golden Harvest Company, Golden Way Films Ltd, Maple Ridge Films

A young man from China visits his uncle and comes up against everyone from thugs to the mob.

Elements:
Martial arts / Wackiness / Gangsters / Friendship

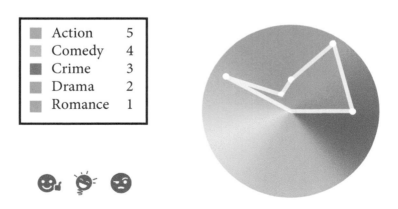

	Action	5
	Comedy	4
	Crime	3
	Drama	2
	Romance	1

"How's that for a slice
of fried gold?"

"Shaun of the Dead" (2004)

Written by Simon Pegg & Edgar Wright
Directed by Edgar Wright

Starring Simon Pegg, Nick Frost, & Kate Ashfield

Universal Pictures, Studio Canal, Working Title Films

A zombie apocalypse causes a recently dumped salesman to kick his life into gear.

Elements:
Parody / Zombies / Breakup / Fight sequence

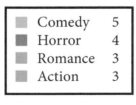

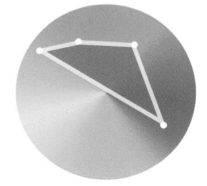

	Comedy	5
	Horror	4
	Romance	3
	Action	3

"Looks like we're
shy one horse."

"*Once Upon a Time in the West*" (1968)

Written by Sergio Donati, Sergio Leone, & Dario Argento
Directed by Sergio Leone

Starring Henry Fonda, Charles Bronson, & Claudia Cardinale

Rafran Cinematografica, San Marco, Paramount Pictures

A mysterious stranger teams up with a gunslinger to protect a widow from an assassin.

Elements:
Cowboys / Shooting / Moral dilemma / Personal enemy / Gangsters / Period setting

	Adventure	5
	Action	3
	Drama	3
	Thriller	2
	Crime	2
	Historical	2

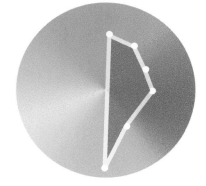

"I didn't come here for
fun or to flirt."

"Frida" (2002)

Written by Hayden Herrera, Clancy Sigal, & Diane Lake
Directed by Julie Taymor

Starring Salma Hayek, Alfred Molina, & Geoffrey Rush

Handprint Entertainment, Lions Gate Films, Miramax

The story of an artist who channels the pain of injury and a turbulent marriage into her work.

Elements:
Real people / Wedding / Society / Traveling / Police

■	Historical	5
■	Romance	4
■	Drama	3
■	Adventure	2
■	Crime	1

"If the moment calls,
give me the phone."

"*Chameleon Street*" (1989)

Written by Wendell B. Harris Jr
Directed by Wendell B. Harris Jr

Starring Timothy Alvaro, Renauld Bailleux, & William Ballenger

Gathsemane 84

Fed up with racial inequality, an ambitious man cons his way into various high stakes professions.

Elements:
Society / Satire / Legality / Identity switch / Real people

■	Drama	5
■	Comedy	3
■	Crime	3
■	Thriller	2
■	Historical	1

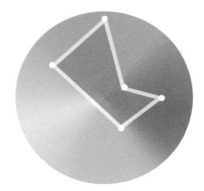

"I hear your voice say
my name when I dream…"

"*Phantom Thread*" (2017)

Written by Paul Thomas Anderson
Directed by Paul Thomas Anderson

Starring Daniel Day-Lewis, Vicky Krieps, & Lesley Manville

Focus Features, Annapurna Pictures, Perfect World Pictures

A renowned dressmaker meets a strong-willed woman who throws his life into disarray.

Elements:
Love interest / Family / Period setting / Ghost / Mystery / Personality clash

Romance	5
Drama	4
Historical	3
Horror	2
Thriller	2
Comedy	1

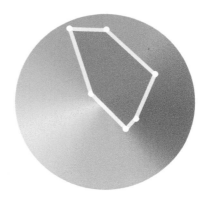

"I'm reviewing the situation..."

"Oliver!" (1968)

Written by Lionel Bart, Vernon Harris, & Charles Dickens
Directed by Carol Reed

Starring Mark Lester, Ron Moody, & Shani Wallis

Romulus Films, Warwick Film Productions

An orphan flees from servitude and joins a gang of pickpockets in Victorian London.

Elements:
Performance / Gangsters / Period setting / Society / Traveling / Brutal killing

Musical	5
Crime	4
Historical	4
Drama	3
Adventure	2
Horror	1

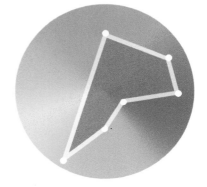

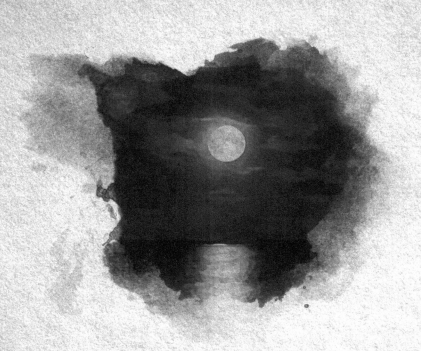

"If you're ever in town
man, holler at me."

"Moonlight" (2016)

Written by Barry Jenkins & Tarell Alvin McCraney
Directed by Barry Jenkins

Starring Mahershala Ali, Naomie Harris, & Trevante Rhodes

A24, PASTEL, Plan B Entertainment

A young black man searches for his identity and
sexuality, while growing up in a crime ridden area.

Elements:
Friendship / Drugs / Love interest / Psychological
suspense / Violence

Drama	5
Crime	4
Romance	3
Thriller	2
Action	1

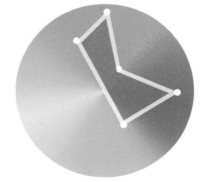

"Grandma was never here."

"*Shoplifters*" (2018)

Written by Hirokazu Koreeda
Directed by Hirokazu Koreeda

Starring Lily Franky, Sakura Ando, & Kirin Kiki

AOI Promotion, Fuji Television Network, Gaga

On the outskirts of Tokyo, a makeshift family of petty criminals are united by loyalty and survival.

Elements:
Society / Legality / Identity switch / Sex / Personality clash

■	Drama	5
■	Crime	3
■	Thriller	3
■	Romance	1
■	Comedy	1

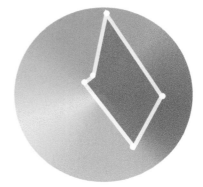

"With the whole world
crumbling… We choose this
time to fall in love."

"*Casablanca*" (1942)

Written by Julius J. Epstein, Philip G. Epstein, & Howard Koch | Directed by Michael Curtiz

Starring Humphrey Bogart, Ingrid Bergman, & Paul Henreid

Warner Bros

An American must decide whether to risk it all and help a young woman escape the Nazis.

Elements:
Love interest / Politics / Moral dilemma / Espionage / Gangsters

■	Romance	5
■	Historical	4
■	Drama	3
■	Thriller	3
■	Crime	2

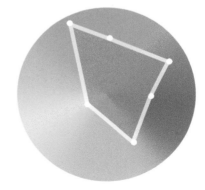

"Sit your raggedy ass down…"

"*Jackie Brown*" (1997)

Written by Elmore Leonard & Quentin Tarantino
Directed by Quentin Tarantino

Starring Pam Grier, Samuel L. Jackson, & Robert Forster

Miramax, A Band Apart, Lawrence Bender Productions

A world-weary flight-attendant is caught in a bind between a drug dealer and the authorities.

Elements:
Gangsters / Moral dilemma / Suspense / Love interest / Shooting / Personality clash

Crime	5
Drama	4
Thriller	3
Romance	2
Action	2
Comedy	1

"I don't shine shoes
any more."

"Goodfellas" (1990)

Written by Nicholas Pileggi & Martin Scorsese
Directed by Martin Scorsese

Starring Robert De Niro, Ray Liotta, & Joe Pesci

Warner Bros

The story of a man who joins the mafia at a young age and grows up being involved in mob activities.

Elements:
Gangsters / Family / Shooting / Suspense / Wittiness / Real people

■	Crime	5
■	Drama	4
■	Action	2
■	Thriller	2
■	Comedy	2
■	Historical	1

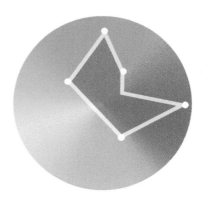

"Who do you got in mind?"

"Ocean's 11" (2001)

Written by George Clayton Johnson, Jack Golden Russell, & Harry Brown | Directed by Steven Soderbergh

Starring George Clooney, Brad Pitt, & Julia Roberts

Warner Bros., Village Roadshow Pictures, NPV Entertainment

A professional thief puts together a team to rob his rival's casinos.

Elements:
Heist / Personal enemy / Wittiness / Violence / Breakup / Teamwork

■	Crime	5
■	Thriller	4
■	Comedy	4
■	Action	2
■	Romance	2
■	Drama	1

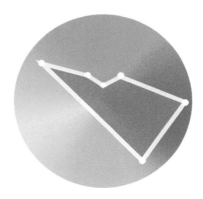

"You need more than guts
to be a good gangster...
You need ideas."

"City of God" (2002)

Written by Paulo Lins & Bráulio Mantovani
Directed by Fernando Meirelles & Kátia Lund

Starring Alexandre Rodrigues, Leandro Firmino, & Matheus Nachtergaele

O2 Filmes, VideoFilmes, Globo Filmes

One boy from the slums of Rio De Janeiro pursues photography, while another adopts a life of crime.

Elements:
Gangsters / Society / Suspense / Shooting / Love interest / Real people

	Crime	5
	Drama	4
	Thriller	3
	Action	2
	Romance	1
	Historical	1

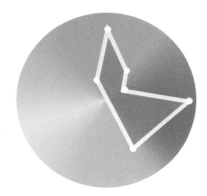

"What we do in life,
echoes in eternity!"

"Gladiator" (2000)

Written by David Franzoni, John Logan, & William
Nicholson | Directed by Ridley Scott

Starring Russell Crowe, Joaquin Phoenix, & Connie Nielsen

Dreamworks Pictures, Universal Pictures, Scott Free Productions

A former Roman general vows revenge against the
ruler who defamed him and killed his family.

Elements:
Period setting / Fight sequence / Quest / Society /
Personal enemy / Gore

▇	Historical	5
▇	Action	4
▇	Adventure	4
▇	Drama	4
▇	Thriller	3
▇	Horror	2

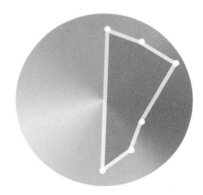

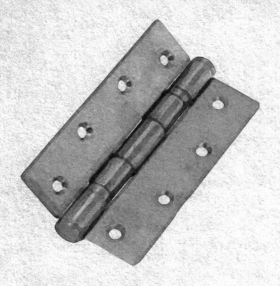

"Power is when we have
every justification to kill
and we don't."

"Schindler's List" (1993)

Written by Thomas Keneally & Steven Zaillian
Directed by Steven Spielberg

Starring Liam Neeson, Ralph Fiennes, & Ben Kingsley

Universal Pictures, Amblin Entertainment

An industrialist is concerned for the safety of his Jewish workforce in Nazi-occupied Poland.

Elements:
Period setting / Society / Brutal killing / Evading authority / Dystopian

▣	Historical	5
▣	Drama	4
▣	Horror	3
▣	Thriller	2
▣	Sci-Fi	1

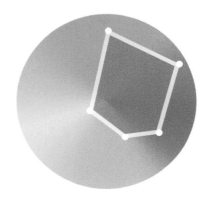

"How you fall doesn't matter,
it's how you land."

"*La Haine*" (1995)

Written by Mathieu Kassovitz
Directed by Mathieu Kassovitz

Starring Vincent Cassel, Hubert Koundé, & Saïd Taghmaoui

Les Productions Lazennec, Le Studio Canal+, La Sept Cinéma

Three young men from the suburbs of Paris face police, violence, and adversity during the riots.

Elements:
Police / Society / Suspense / Shooting / Politics

■	Crime	5
■	Drama	4
■	Thriller	2
■	Action	1
■	Historical	1

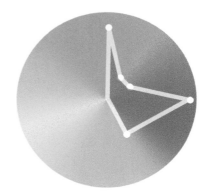

"It's like looking for a needle
in a stack of needles."

"*Saving Private Ryan*" (1998)

Written by Robert Rodat
Directed by Steven Spielberg

Starring Tom Hanks, Matt Damon, & Tom Sizemore

Dreamworks Pictures, Paramount Pictures, Amblin Entertainment

A squad of soldiers attempt to rescue a mother's last surviving son from behind enemy lines.

Elements:
Shooting / Period setting / Gore / Suspense / Teamwork / Quest

■	Action	5
■	Historical	4
■	Horror	3
■	Thriller	3
■	Drama	3
■	Adventure	2

"A real doggone keeper?"

"Get Out" (2017)

Written by Jordan Peele
Directed by Jordan Peele

Starring Daniel Kaluuya, Allison Williams, & Bradley Whitford

Universal Pictures, Blumhouse Productions, QC Entertainment

A black man goes to meet his white girlfriend's family and discovers their sinister secret.

Elements:
Confined setting / Identity switch / Society / Love interest / Wittiness

	Horror	5
	Thriller	4
	Drama	3
	Romance	3
	Comedy	2

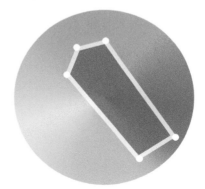

"I don't want to survive,
I want to live."

"12 Years a Slave" (2013)

Written by John Ridley & Solomon Northup
Directed by Steve McQueen

Starring Chiwetel Ejiofor, Michael Kenneth Williams, & Michael Fassbender

New Regency Productions, River Road Entertainment, Plan B Entertainment

Before the American civil war, a free man is abducted and sold into slavery.

Elements:
Real people / Society / Torture / Identity switch / Legality / Quest

■	Historical	5
■	Drama	4
■	Horror	3
■	Thriller	3
■	Crime	2
■	Adventure	1

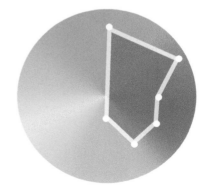

"Okay."

"*Scarface*" (1983)

Written by Oliver Stone, Howard Hawks, & Ben Hecht
Directed by Brian De Palma

Starring Al Pacino, Michelle Pfeiffer, & Steven Bauer

Universal Pictures

A headstrong Cuban immigrant takes over the cartels, to the detriment of everyone around him.

Elements:
Gangsters / Shooting / Psychological suspense / Gore / Society / True events

■ Crime	5
■ Action	4
■ Thriller	3
■ Horror	3
■ Drama	2
■ Historical	1

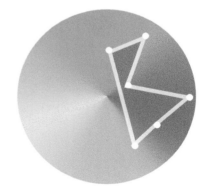

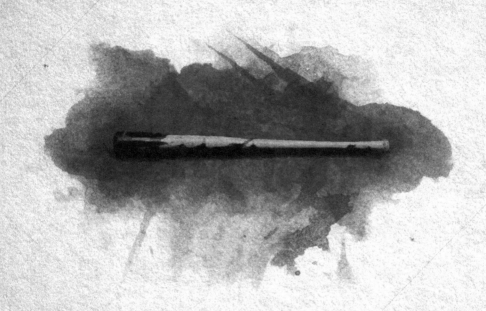

"I'll take you to Mom,
no matter what."

"*Train to Busan*" (2016)

Written by Joo-Suk Park & Sang-Ho Yeon
Directed by Sang-Ho Yeon

Starring Gong Yoo, Jung Yu-mi, & Ma Dong-seok

Next Entertainment World (NEW), RedPeter Film, Movic Comics

When a zombie virus sweeps South Korea, a group of people try to survive on a train.

Elements:
Zombies / Fight sequence / Suspense / Family

Horror	5
Action	4
Thriller	4
Drama	2

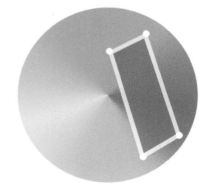

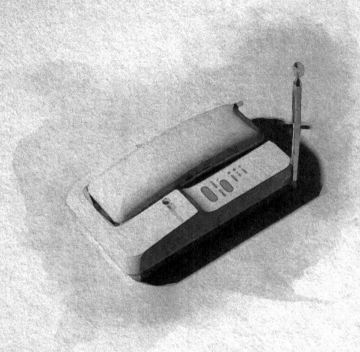

"Why don't you wanna
talk to me?"

"Scream" (1996)

Written by Kevin Williamson
Directed by Wes Craven

Starring Neve Campbell, Courteney Cox, & David Arquette

Dimension Films, Woods Entertainment

After her mother's murder, a teenage girl is stalked by a masked killer who is inspired by horror movies.

Elements:
Brutal killing / Suspense / Friendship / Love interest / Satire

■	Horror	5
■	Thriller	3
■	Drama	2
■	Romance	1
■	Comedy	1

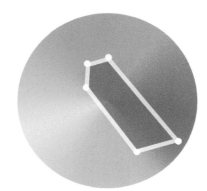

"If it bleeds, we can kill it."

"Predator" (1987)

Written by Jim Thomas & John Thomas
Directed by John McTiernan

Starring Arnold Schwarzenegger, Carl Weathers, & Kevin Peter Hall

Twentieth Century Fox, Lawrence Gordon Productions, Silver Pictures

A team of commandos in a South-American jungle
are hunted by an extra terrestrial killer.

Elements:
Shooting / Impending doom / Mystery / Quest /
Extra terrestrial

■	Action	5
■	Horror	4
■	Thriller	3
■	Adventure	2
■	Sci-Fi	1

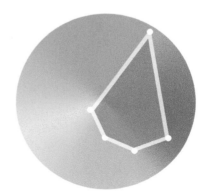

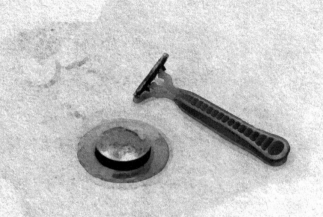

"Go get a cane-pole.
Catch the fish that ate him."

"The Fugitive" (1993)

Written by Jeb Stuart, David Twohy, & Roy Huggins
Directed by Andrew Davis

Starring Harrison Ford, Tommy Lee Jones, & Sela Ward

Warner Bros, Kopelson Entertainment

A doctor is falsely accused of murder and must track down the real killer while evading the law.

Elements:
Evading authority / Car chase / Police / Traveling

Thriller	5
Action	4
Crime	3
Adventure	1

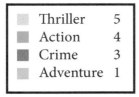

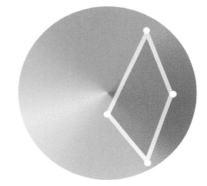

"Better to be a fake somebody
than a real nobody."

"The Talented Mr Ripley" (1999)

Written by Patricia Highsmith & Anthony Minghella
Directed by Anthony Minghella

Starring Matt Damon, Gwyneth Paltrow, & Jude Law

Miramax, Paramount Pictures, Mirage Enterprises

A young underachiever sets out to retrieve a millionnaire's son but ends up obsessed with him.

Elements:
Identity switch / Legality / Love interest /
Friendship / Traveling

Thriller	5
Crime	4
Romance	2
Drama	2
Adventure	1

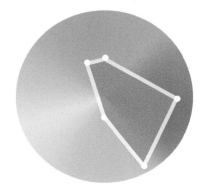

"It puts the lotion
on its skin…"

"*The Silence of the Lambs*" (1991)

Written by Thomas Harris & Ted Tally
Directed by Jonathan Demme

Starring Jodie Foster, Anthony Hopkins, & Lawrence A. Bonney

Strong Heart/Demme Production, Orion Pictures

An F.B.I. agent seeks the help of a psychopathic cannibal to help her stop a serial killer.

Elements:
Psychological suspense / Gore / Police / Society

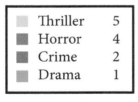

Thriller	5
Horror	4
Crime	2
Drama	1

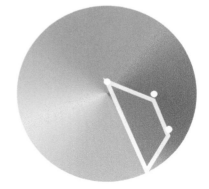

"You probably know as much about possession as most priests."

"The Exorcist" (1973)

Written by William Peter Blatty
Directed by William Friedkin

Starring Ellen Burstyn, Max von Sydow, & Linda Blair

Warner Bros, Hoya Productions

When a young girl is possessed by a mysterious entity, her mother seeks the help of a priest.

Elements:
Possession / Mystery / Family / Experimental technology

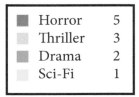

■ Horror	5
▫ Thriller	3
■ Drama	2
▫ Sci-Fi	1

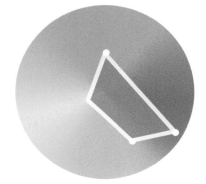

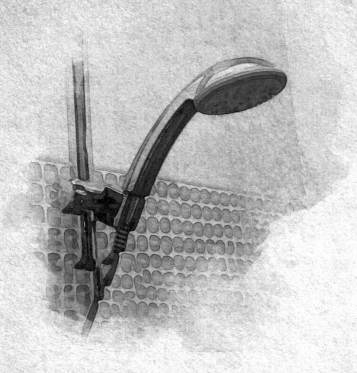

"We all go a little mad
sometimes."

"Psycho" (1960)

Written by Joseph Stefano & Robert Bloch
Directed by Alfred Hitchcock

Starring Anthony Perkins, Janet Leigh, & Vera Miles

Shamley Productions

A woman on the run stops over at a motel which is
run by the son of a domineering mother.

Elements:
Psychological suspense / Brutal killing / Police /
Love interest / Family

Thriller	5
Horror	3
Crime	2
Romance	2
Drama	1

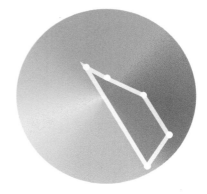

"It's been a great pleasure
meeting a Christian copper."

"*The Wicker Man*" (1973)

Written by Anthony Shaffer & David Pinner
Directed by Robin Hardy

Starring Edward Woodward, Christopher Lee, & Diane Cilento

British Lion Film Corporation

A policeman searches for a missing girl on an island where the locals claim she never existed.

Elements:
Cult / Mystery / Society / Performance / Inconquerable terrain

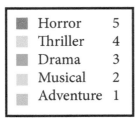

Horror	5
Thriller	4
Drama	3
Musical	2
Adventure	1

"I'm so much happier
now that I'm dead."

"Gone Girl" (2014)

Written by Gillian Flynn
Directed by David Fincher

Starring Ben Affleck, Rosamund Pike, & Neil Patrick Harris

Twentieth Century Fox, New Regency Productions, TSG Entertainment

The media frenzy surrounding a woman's disappearance lands her husband in hot water.

Elements:
Psychological suspense / Breakup / Society / Police

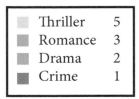

Thriller	5
Romance	3
Drama	2
Crime	1

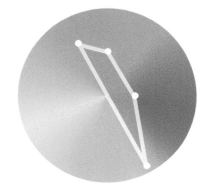

"I'm not real enough for you?"

"*It*" (2017)

Written by Chase Palmer, Cary Joji Fukunaga, & Gary Dauberman | Directed by Andy Muschietti

Starring Bill Skarsgård, Jaeden Martell, & Finn Wolfhard

New Line Cinema, RatPac-Dune Entertainment, Vertigo Entertainment

A group of kids investigate a monster appearing as an evil clown. Based on the Stephen King novel.

Elements:
Monster / Treasure hunt / Mystery / Friendship

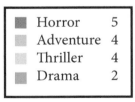

■ Horror	5
■ Adventure	4
■ Thriller	4
■ Drama	2

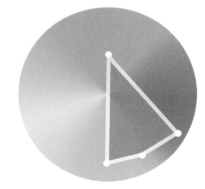

"A surgeon never kills a patient."

"The Killing of a Sacred Deer" (2018)

Written by Yorgos Lanthimos & Efthimis Filippou
Directed by Yorgos Lanthimos

Starring Barry G. Bernson, Herb Caillouet, & Bill Camp

Element Pictures, A24, Film4

A surgeon develops a bond with a boy whose intentions become darkly sinister.

Elements:
Mystery / Impending doom / Family / Romantic tension / Myth

▧	Thriller	5
■	Horror	4
◼	Drama	3
▨	Romance	2
▧	Fantasy	2

"Nazis... I hate these guys."

"Indiana Jones and the Last Crusade" (1989)

Written by Jeffrey Boam, George Lucas, & Menno Meyjes
Directed by Stevel Spielberg

Starring Harrison Ford, Sean Connery, & Alison Doody

Paramount Pictures, Lucasfilm

The archeological professor and his father must find the holy grail before the Nazis exploit its powers.

Elements:
Treasure hunt / Personal enemy / Fight sequence / Period setting / Wittiness / Myth / Brutal killing

 Adventure	5	
Thriller	4	
Action	3	
Historical	3	
Comedy	1	
Fantasy	1	
Horror	1	

"We spared no expense."

"*Jurassic Park*" (1993)

Written by Michael Crichton & David Koepp
Directed by Steven Spielberg

Starring Sam Neill, Laura Dern, & Jeff Goldblum

Universal Pictures, Amblin Entertainment

A paleontologist must protect two children from dinosaurs on the loose.

Elements:
Experimental technology / Extreme setting / Physical destruction / Monster / Suspense / Personality clash

Sci-Fi	5
Adventure	4
Action	3
Horror	3
Thriller	2
Comedy	1

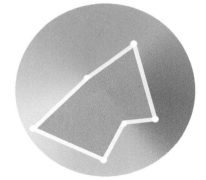

"You mustn't be afraid to
dream a little bigger, darling."

"Inception" (2010)

Written by Christopher Nolan
Directed by Christopher Nolan

Starring Leonardo DiCaprio, Joseph Gordon-Levitt, & Elliot Page

Warner Bros, Legendary Entertainment, Syncopy

A thief's mission to implant an idea via dreams is threatened by his own inner demons.

Elements:
Experimental technology / Shooting / Psychological suspense / Quest / Imaginary world / Heist

Sci-Fi	5
Action	4
Thriller	4
Adventure	3
Fantasy	1
Crime	1

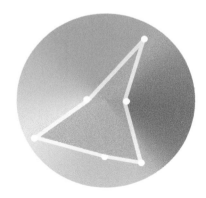

"We live or we die
by the clock."

"Cast Away" (2000)

Written by William Broyles Jr.
Directed by Robert Zemeckis

Starring Tom Hanks, Helen Hunt, & Paul Sanchez

Twentieth Century Fox, Dreamworks Pictures, ImageMovers

A FedEx executive undergoes an emotional journey when he is stranded on a deserted island.

Elements:
Inconquerable terrain / Society / Breakup / Psychological suspense / Surrealism

Adventure	5
Drama	3
Romance	2
Thriller	2
Fantasy	1

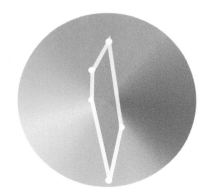

"I have a feeling we're
not in Kansas any more."

"The Wizard of Oz" (1939)

Written by Noel Langley, Florence Ryerson, & Edgar Allan Woolf | Directed by Victor Fleming, George Cukor, & Mervyn LeRoy

Starring Judy Garland, Frank Morgan, & Ray Bolger

Metro-Goldwyn-Mayer (MGM)

A girl from Kansas enters a magical world and must find a wizard who can get her home.

Elements:
Performance / Imaginary world / Quest / Personality clash / Monster

	Musical	5
	Fantasy	4
	Adventure	4
	Comedy	3
	Horror	2

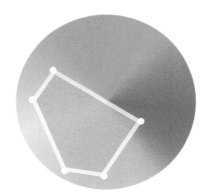

"Doubt is useful. It keeps
faith a living thing."

"Life of Pi" (1996)

Written by Yann Martel & David Magee
Directed by Ang Lee

Starring Suraj Sharma, Irrfan Khan, & Adil Hussain

Fox 2000 Pictures, Dune Entertainment, Ingenious Media

A young boy finds himself adrift on a small boat with a tiger, whom he names Richard Parker.

Elements:
Quest / Society / Imaginary world / Confined setting / Irony

▪	Adventure	5
▪	Fantasy	3
▪	Drama	2
▪	Horror	1
▪	Comedy	1

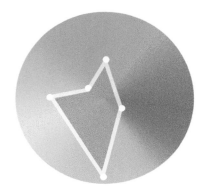

"The ones that love us
never really leave us."

"Harry Potter and the Prisoner of Azkaban" (2004)

Written by J.K. Rowling & Steve Kloves
Directed by Alfonso Cuarón

Starring Daniel Radcliffe, Emma Watson, & Rupert Grint

Warner Bros, 1492 Pictures, Heyday Films

An escaped convict poses a threat to students at Hogwarts school of witchcraft and wizardry.

Elements:
Magic / Treasure hunt / Friendship / Identity switch / Monster

	Fantasy	5
	Adventure	4
	Drama	3
	Thriller	2
	Horror	1

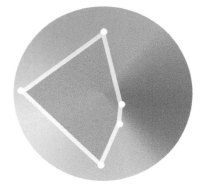

"It's very dangerous up
there amongst the beans."

"*The Borrowers*" (1997)

Written by Mary Norton, Gavin Scott, & John Kamps
Directed by Peter Hewitt

Starring John Goodman, Jim Broadbent, & Mark Williams

Polygram Filmed Entertainment, Working Title Films

A secret family of 4-inch tall people try to save their home from an evil housing-developer.

Elements:
Extreme setting / Surrealism / Absurdity / Family / Suspense

■	Adventure	5
■	Fantasy	4
■	Comedy	3
■	Drama	2
■	Thriller	1

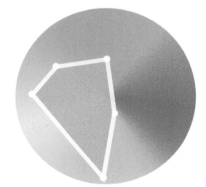

"There is no spoon."

"The Matrix" (1999)

Written by Lilly Wachowski & Lana Wachowski
Directed by Lilly Wachowski & Lana Wachowski

Starring Keanu Reeves, Laurence Fishburne, & Carrie-Anne Moss

Warner Bros. Village Roadshow Pictures, Groucho Film Partnership

A cyber-hacker discovers that reality is a simulation and must fight to save the human race.

Elements:
Artificial intelligence / Martial arts / Suspense / Love interest / Quest

	Sci-Fi	5
	Action	4
	Thriller	4
	Romance	2
	Adventure	2

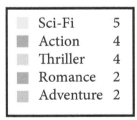

"Hasta la vista, baby."

"Terminator 2: Judgement Day" (1991)

Written by James Cameron & William Wisher
Directed by James Cameron

Starring Arnold Schwarzenegger, Linda Hamilton, & Edward Furlong

Carolco Pictures, Pacific Western, Lightstorm Entertainment

An unstoppable cyborg is sent from the future to kill the leader of the human resistance as a child.

Elements:
Time travel / Fight sequence / Personal enemy / Quest / Family

Sci-Fi	5
Action	4
Thriller	4
Adventure	2
Drama	1

"Houston, we have a problem."

"Apollo 13" (1995)

Written by Jim Lovell, Jeffrey Kluger, & William Broyles Jr.
Directed by Ron Howard

Starring Tom Hanks, Bill Paxton, & Kevin Bacon

Universal Pictures, Imagine Entertainment

A NASA spacecraft is damaged and the astronauts on board must undergo a perilous return to earth.

Elements:
Real people / Space travel / Suspense / Quest / Family

■	Historical	5
▫	Sci-Fi	4
▨	Thriller	3
▨	Adventure	3
■	Drama	1

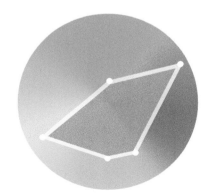

"For years, we've been trying
to combine the bloodlines."

"*Underworld*" (2003)

Written by Kevin Grevioux, Len Wiseman, & Danny McBride
| Directed by Len Wiseman

Starring Kate Beckinsale, Scott Speedman, & Shane Brolly

Lakeshore Entertainment, Screen Gems, Subterranean Productions UK Ltd.

In the midst of a blood feud with werewolves, a vampire falls in love with a human.

Elements:
Strange creatures / Fight sequence / Mystery / Quest / Love interest / Confined setting

	Fantasy	5
	Action	4
	Thriller	4
	Adventure	3
	Romance	2
	Horror	1

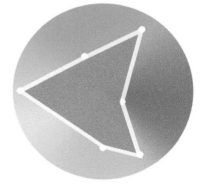

"It's the size of a house!"

"Honey, I Shrunk the Kids" (1989)

Written by Stuart Gordon, Brian Yuzna, & Ed Naha
Directed by Joe Johnston

Starring Rick Moranis, Matt Frewer, & Marcia Strassman

Walt Disney Pictures, Silver Screen Partners III, Doric Productions

An inventor accidentally shrinks his children and their friends, who end up lost in the garden.

Elements:
Inconquerable terrain / Wackiness / Experimental technology / Family / Love interest

■	Adventure	5
■	Comedy	4
■	Sci-Fi	3
■	Drama	2
■	Romance	1

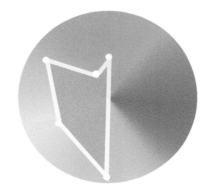

"You better believe it,
and I'm loaded with both."

"*The Jungle Book*" (1967)

Written by Larry Clemmons, Ralph Wright, & Ken Anderson
Directed by Wolfgang Reitherman

Starring Phil Harris, Sebastian Cabot, & Louis Prima

Walt Disney Animation Studios

A paternal panther and an avuncular bear struggle to persuade a young boy to return to human society.

Elements:
Performance / Inconquerable terrain / Surrealism / Absurdity / Friendship

Musical	5
Adventure	4
Fantasy	4
Comedy	3
Drama	3

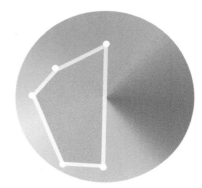

Why not create a unique colour code for your favourite movie? Just tally the elements, then use an online colour calculator and follow the formula below:

Drama = ff0000
Action = ff0080
Historical = ff00ff
Crime = 8000ff
Horror = 0000ff
Thriller = 00ffff
Adventure = 00ff00
Musical = abff00
Sci-Fi = ffff00
Fantasy = ffff00
Comedy = ff8000
Romance = ff4000

E.g. Comedy 3 Romance 2 Drama 1
ff8000 + ff8000 + ff8000
+ ff4000 + ff4000 + ff0000
=
#ff5500

Acknowledgements

I would like to thank Shmuel Barber and Dan Christie for their helpful comments, everyone who assisted with the launch, my friends Adrian Kwan and Hannah Chang for their support, my mother for her hospitality during the writing process, and my uncle Andrew Bethell for his encouragement over the years.

I am grateful to all my teachers, past and present, and to the publishers for enabling me to put some of what I have learned into a book. I should also commend the meticulous proofreading done by Luke Palder of Proofreadingservices.com. A debt of gratitude is also owed to the plethora of filmmakers from around the world whose works I have cited.

Not only this, but I also thank you, dear reader. I hope you enjoyed this book. If so, please recommend it or, better yet, leave a review online. I am a filmmaker, and all proceeds will be invested in creative projects.

My hope is that, by understanding how genre affects emotion, everyone can feel inspired and empowered to make a freer choice regarding what they watch. Rather than following the algorithm towards emotional numbness, prioritising one's emotional state grants a symbiotic connection with the artist and indeed the art.

Although I have said a lot about my family, I will add one final thing; my maternal ancestry includes the renowned painter and abolitionist J.M.W. Turner. His dramatic seascapes depicted, among other things, the horrors of the transatlantic slave trade. Publicising the cruel reality of slavery was a way of protesting and supporting its abolition.

A picture speaks a thousand words; Turner's paintings told a horrific story through colour, and his storytelling was revolutionary. Therefore, we should recognise the usefulness of colour for summoning emotions within everyone from members of the general public to the king. If we could learn but one thing from Turner, we ought to learn that colour is the key to communication. His oil paintings and watercolour pieces were stupendously vibrant and used distinct colour palettes to elicit emotions from viewers. This suggests that he carefully considered the genre of his paintings. Nowadays, the most prolific media are film & T.V., so we should apply this understanding to those media, as they also have the power to change the world in their own way.

Filmography

Pg. 3 – *Titanic* (1997), starring: Leonardo DiCaprio, Kate Winslet, Billy Zane / Writer: James Cameron / Director: James Cameron / Production companies: Twentieth Century Fox, Paramount Pictures, Lightstorm Entertainment

Pg. 8 – *The House of the Devil* (1896), original title: *Le Manoir du Diable* / Starring: Jehanne d'Alcy, Jules-Eugène Legris, Georges Méliès / Writer: Georges Méliès / Director: Georges Méliès / Production companies: Georges Méliès, Star-Film

Pg. 8 – *A Trip to the Moon* (1902), original title: *Le Voyage dans la Lune* / Starring: Georges Méliès, Victor André, Bleuette Bernon / Writers: Georges Méliès, Jules Verne, & H.G. Wells / Director: Georges Méliès / Production company: Star-Film

Pg. 13 – *Super Troopers* (2001), starring: Jay Chandrasekhar, Kevin Heffernan, André Vippolis / Writers: Jay Chandrasekhar, Kevin Heffernan, & Steve Lemme / Director: Jay Chandrasekhar / Production companies: Searchlight Pictures, Jersey Shore, Cataland Films

Pg. 13 – *Detroit* (2017), starring: John Boyega, Anthony Mackie, Algee Smith, Will Poulter / Writer: Mark Boal / Director: Kathryn Bigelow / Production companies: Annapurna Pictures, First Light Production, Page 1

Pg. 16 – *Whiplash* (2014), starring: Miles Teller, J.K. Simmons, Melissa Benoist / Writer: Damien Chazelle / Director: Damien Chazelle / Production companies: Bold Films, Blumhouse Productions, Right of Way Films

Pg. 23 – *Ghostbusters* (1984), starring: Bill Murray, Dan Aykroyd, Sigourney Weaver / Writers: Dan Aykroyd, Harold Ramis & Rick Moranis / Director: Ivan Reitman / Production companies: Columbia Pictures, Delphi Films, Black Rhino Productions

Pg. 23 – *Vertigo* (1958), starring: James Stewart, Kim Novak, Barbara Bel Geddes / Writers: Alec Coppel, Samuel A. Taylor, & Pierre Boileau / Director: Alfred Hitchcock / Production company: Alfred J. Hitchcock Productions

Pg. 23 – *Easy Rider* (1969), starring: Peter Fonda, Dennis Hopper, Jack Nicholson / Writers: Peter Fonda, Dennis Hopper, & Terry Southern / Director: Dennis Hopper / Production companies: Pando Company Inc., Raybert Productions

Pg. 23 – *Holes* (2003), starring: Shia LaBeouf, Sigourney Weaver, Jon Voight / Writer: Louis Sachar / Director: Andrew Davis / Production companies: Walt Disney Pictures, Walden Media, Chicago Pacific Entertainment

Pg. 25 – *2001: A Space Odyssey* (1968), starring: Keir Dullea, Gary Lockwood, William Sylvester / Writers: Stanley Kubrick, & Arthur C. Clarke / Director: Stanley Kubrick / Production companies: Metro-Goldwyn-Mayer (MGM), Stanley Kubrick Productions

Pg. 25 – *John Wick* (2014), starring: Keanu Reeves, Michael Nyqvist, Alfie Allen / Writer: Derek Kolstad / Directors: Chad Stahelski & David Leitch / Production companies: Summit Entertainment, Thunder Road Pictures, 87Eleven

Pg. 39 – *The Hitchhiker's Guide to the Galaxy* (2005), starring: Martin Freeman, Yasiin Bey, Sam Rockwell / Writers: Douglas Adams & Karey Kirkpatrick / Director: Garth Jennings / Production companies: Touchstone Pictures, Spyglass Entertainment, Everyman Pictures

Pg. 41 — *Jumanji* (1995), starring: Robin Williams, Kirsten Dunst, Bonnie Hunt / Writers: Jonathan Hensleigh, Greg Taylor, & Jim Strain / Director: Joe Johnston / Production companies: TriStar Pictures, Interscope Communications, Teitler Film

Pg. 43 — *Star Wars: Episode V - The Empire Strikes Back* (1980), starring: Mark Hamill, Harrison Ford, Carrie Fisher / Writers: Leigh Brackett, Lawrence Kasdan, & George Lucas / Director: Irvin Kershner / Production Company: Lucasfilm

Pg. 45 — *The Lord of the Rings: The Two Towers* (2002), starring: Elijah Wood, Ian McKellen, Viggo Mortensen / Writers: J.R.R. Tolkien, Fran Walsh, & Philippa Boyens / Director: Peter Jackson / Production companies: New Line Cinema, WingNut Films, The Saul Zaentz Company

Pg. 47 — *Everything Everywhere All At Once* (2022), starring: Michelle Yeoh, Stephanie Hsu, Jamie Lee Curtis / Writers: Daniel Kwan & Daniel Scheinert / Directors: Daniel Kwan & Daniel Scheinert / Production companies: A24, IAC Films, AGBO

Pg. 49 — *Princess Mononoke* (1997), original title: *Mononoke-Hime* / Starring: Yôji Matsuda, Yuriko Ishida, Yûko Tanaka / Writers: Hayao Miyazaki & Neil Gaiman / Director: Hayao Miyazaki / Production companies: DENTSU Music And Entertainment, Nibariki, Nippon Television Network (NTV)

Pg. 51 — *Spiderman 2* (2004) starring: Tobey Maguire, Kirsten Dunst, Alfred Molina / Writers: Stan Lee, Steve Ditko, & Alfred Gough / Director: Sam Raimi / Production companies: Columbia Pictures, Marvel Enterprises, Laura Ziskin Productions

Pg. 53 — *Moulin Rouge!* (2001), starring: Nicole Kidman, Ewan McGregor, John Leguizamo / Writers: Baz Luhrmann & Craig Pearce / Director: Baz Luhrmann / Production companies: Twentieth Century Fox, Bazmark Films

Pg. 55 — *Shrek* (2001), starring: Mike Myers, Eddie Murphy, Cameron Diaz / Writers: William Steig, Ted Elliott, & Terry Rossio / Directors: Andrew Adamson & Vicky Jenson / Production companies: DreamWorks Animation, Dreamworks Pictures, Pacific Data Images (PDI)

Pg. 57 — *Dumb and Dumber* (1994), starring: Jim Carrey, Jeff Daniels, Lauren Holly / Writers: Peter Farrelly, Bennett Yellin, & Bobby Farrelly / Directors: Peter Farrelly & Bobby Farrelly / Production companies: New Line Cinema, Motion Picture Corporation of America (MPCA)

Pg. 59 — *Her* (2013), starring: Joaquin Phoenix, Amy Adams, Scarlett Johansson / Writer: Spiike Jonze / Director: Spike Jonze / Production companies: Annapurna Pictures, Stage 6 Films

Pg. 61 — *PK* (2014), starring: Aamir Khan, Anushka Sharma, Sanjay Dutt / Writers: Rajkumar Hirani & Abhijat Joshi / Director: Rajkumar Hirani / Production companies: Rajkumar Hirani Films, Vinod Chopra Productions

Pg. 63 — *Little Miss Sunshine* (2006), starring: Steve Carell, Toni Collette, Greg Kinnear / Writer: Michael Arndt / Directors: Jonathan Dayton & Valerie Faris / Production companies: Searchlight Pictures, Big Beach Films, Bona Fide Productions

Pg. 65 — *Force Majeure* (2014), original title: *Turist* / Starring: Johannes Kuhnke, Lisa Loven Kongsli, Clara Wettergren / Writer: Ruben Östlund / Director: Ruben Östlund / Production companies: Plattform Produktion, Film i Väst, Rhône-Alpes Cinéma

Pg. 67 — *Brokeback Mountain* (2005), starring: Jake Gyllenhaal, Heath Ledger, Michelle Williams / Writers: Annie Proulx, Larry McMurtry, & Diana Ossana / Director: Ang Lee / Production companies: Focus Features, River Road Entertainment, Alberta Film Entertainment

Pg. 69 — *Amélie* (2001), original title: *Le Fabuleux Destin d'Amélie Poulain* / Starring: Audrey Tautou, Mathieu Kassovitz & Rufus / Writers: Guillaume Laurant & Jean-Pierre Jeunet / Director: Jean-Pierre Jeunet / Production companies: Claudie Ossard Productions, Union Générale Cinématographique (UGC), Victoires Productions

Pg. 71 – *Bridesmaids* (2011), starring: Kristen Wiig, Maya Rudolph, Rose Byrne / Writers: Kristen Wiig & Annie Mumolo / Director: Paul Feig / Production companies: Universal Pictures, Relativity Media, Apatow Productions

Pg. 73 – *God of Cookery* (1996), original title: *Sik San* / Starring: Stephen Chow, Karen Mok, Vincent Kok / Writers: Stephen Chow, Man-Sang Lo, & Kan-Cheung Tsang / Directors: Stephen Chow & Lik-Chi Lee / Production company: Star Overseas

Pg. 75 – *Rain Man* (1988), starring: Dustin Hoffman, Tom Cruise, Valeria Golino / Writers: Barry Morrow & Ron Bass / Director: Barry Levinson / Production companies: United Artists, The Guber-Peters Company, Star Partners II Ltd.

Pg. 77 – *The Mask of Zorro* (1998), starring: Antonio Banderas, Anthony Hopkins, Catherine Zeta-Jones / Writers: Johnston McCulley, Ted Elliott, & Terry Rossio / Director: Martin Campbell / Production companies: TriStar Pictures, Amblin Entertainment, David Foster Productions

Pg. 79 – *Sorry to Bother You* (2018), starring: LaKeith Stanfield, Tessa Thompson, Jermaine Fowler / Writer: Boots Riley / Director: Boots Riley / Production companies: Cinereach, MACROMNM Creative

Pg. 81 – *Monty Python's Life of Brian* (1979), starring: Graham Chapman, John Cleese, Michael Palin / Writers: Graham Chapman, John Cleese, & Terry Gilliam / Director: Terry Jones / Production companies: HandMade Films, Python (Monty) Pictures

Pg. 83 – *Les Misérables* (2012), starring: Hugh Jackman, Russell Crowe, Anne Hathaway / Writers: William Nicholson, Alain Boublil, & Claude-Michel Schönberg / Director: Tom Hooper / Production companies: Universal Pictures, Working Title Films, Cameron Mackintosh Ltd.

Pg. 85 – *The Notebook* (2004), starring: Ryan Gosling, Rachel McAdams, Gena Rowlands, James Garner / Writers: Jeremy Leven, Jan Sardi & Nicholas Sparks / Director: Nick Cassavetes / Production companies: New Line Cinema, Gran Via Productions, Avery Pix

Pg. 87 – *Hidden Figures* (2016), starring: Taraji P. Henson, Octavia Spencer, Janelle Monáe / Writers: Allison Schroeder, Theodore Melfi, & Margot Lee Shetterly / Director: Theodore Melfi / Production companies: Fox 2000 Pictures, Chernin Entertainment, Levantine Films

Pg. 89 – *Little Big Master* (2015), original title: *Ng goh Siu hai dik hau Jeung* / Starring: Miriam Chin Wah Yeung, Louis Koo, Winnie Yuen-Ying Ho / Writers: Hannah Chang & Adrian Kwan / Director: Adrian Kwan / Production companies: One Cool Film Production, Sil-Metropole Organisation, Sirius Pictures International

Pg. 91 – *Pan's Labyrinth* (2006), original title: *El Laberinto del Fauno* / Starring: Ivana Baquero, Ariadna Gil, Sergi López / Writer: Guillermo Del Toro / Director: Guillermo Del Toro / Production companies: Tequila Gang, Estudios Picasso, Esperanto Filmoj

Pg. 93 – *Cool Hand Luke* (1967), starring: Paul Newman, George Kennedy, Strother Martin / Writers: Donn Pearce, Frank Pierson, & Hal Dresner / Director: Stuart Rosenberg / Production company: Jalem Productions

Pg. 95 – *Rumble in the Bronx* (1995), original title: *Hung Fan Kui* / Starring: Jackie Chan, Anita Mui, Françoise Yip / Writers: Edward Tang & Fibe Ma / Director: Stanley Tong / Production companies: Golden Harvest Company, Golden Way Films Ltd., Maple Ridge Films

Pg. 97 – *Shaun of the Dead* (2004), starring: Simon Pegg, Nick Frost, Kate Ashfield / Writers: Simon Pegg & Edgar Wright / Director: Edgar Wright / Production companies: Universal Pictures, StudioCanal, Working Title Films

Pg. 99 – *Once Upon a Time in the West* (1968), starring: Henry Fonda, Charles Bronson, Claudia Cardinale / Writers: Sergio Donati, Sergio Leone, & Dario Argento / Director: Sergio Leone / Production companies: Rafran Cinematografica, San Marco, Paramount Pictures

Pg. 101 — *Frida* (2002), starring: Salma Hayek, Alfred Molina, Geoffrey Rush / Writers: Hayden Herrera, Clancy Sigal, & Diane Lake / Director: Julie Taymor / Production companies: Handprint Entertainment, Lions Gate Films, Miramax

Pg. 103 — *Chameleon Street* (1989), starring: Timothy Alvaro, Renauld Bailleux, William Ballenger / Writer: Wendell B. Harris Jr. / Director: Wendell B. Harris Jr. / Production company: Gathsemane 84

Pg. 105 — *Phantom Thread* (2017), starring: Daniel Day-Lewis, Vicky Krieps, Lesley Manville / Writer: Paul Thomas Anderson / Director: Paul Thomas Anderson / Production companies: Focus Features, Annapurna Pictures, Perfect World Pictures

Pg. 107 — *Oliver!* (1968), starring: Mark Lester, Ron Moody, Shani Wallis / Writers: Lionel Bart, Vernon Harris, & Charles Dickens / Director: Carol Reed / Production companies: Romulus Films, Warwick Film Productions

Pg. 109 — *Moonlight* (2016), starring: Mahershala Ali, Naomie Harris, Trevante Rhodes / Writers: Barry Jenkins & Tarell Alvin McCraney / Director: Barry Jenkins / Production companies: A24, PASTEL, Plan B Entertainment

Pg. 111 — *Shoplifters* (2018), original title: *Manbiki Kazoku* / Starring: Lily Franky, Sakura Ando, Kirin Kiki / Writer: Hirokazu Koreeda / Director: Hirozaku Koreeda / Production companies: AOI Promotion, Fuji Television Network, Gaga

Pg. 113 — *Casablanca* (1942), starring: Humphrey Bogart, Ingrid Bergman, Paul Henreid / Writers: Julius J. Epstein, Philip G. Epstein, & Howard Koch / Director: Michael Curtiz / Production company: Warner Bros.

Pg. 115 — *Jackie Brown* (1997), starring: Pam Grier, Samuel L. Jackson, Robert Forster / Writers: Quentin Tarantino & Elmore Leonard / Director: Quentin Tarantino / Production companies: Miramax, A Band Apart, Lawrence Bender Productions

Pg. 117 — *Goodfellas* (1990), starring: Robert De Niro, Ray Liotta, Joe Pesci / Writers: Nicholas Pileggi & Martin Scorsese / Director: Martin Scorcese / Production company: Warner Bros.

Pg. 119 — *Oceans 11* (2001), starring: George Clooney, Brad Pitt, Julia Roberts / Writers: George Clayton Johnson, Jack Golden Russell & Harry Brown / Director: Steven Soderbergh / Production companies: Warner Bros., Village Roadshow Pictures & NPV Entertainment

Pg. 121 — *City of God* (2002), original title: *Cidade de Deus* / Starring: Alexandre Rodrigues, Leandro Firmino, Matheus Nachtergaele / Writers: Paulo Lins & Bráulio Mantovani / Directors: Fernando Meirelles & Kátia Lund / Production companies: O2 Filmes, VideoFilmes, Globo Filmes

Pg. 123 — *Gladiator* (2000), starring: Russell Crowe, Joaquin Phoenix, Connie Nielsen / Writers: David Franzoni, John Logan, & William Nicholson / Director: Ridley Scott / Production companies: Dreamworks Pictures, Universal Pictures, Scott Free Productions

Pg. 125 — *Schindler's List* (1993), starring: Liam Neeson, Ralph Fiennes, Ben Kingsley / Writers: Thomas Keneally & Steven Zaillian / Director: Steven Spielberg / Production companies: Universal Pictures, Amblin Entertainment

Pg. 127 — *La Haine* (1995), starring: Vincent Cassel, Hubert Koundé, Saïd Taghmaoui / Writer: Mathieu Kassovitz / Director: Mathieu Kassovitz / Production companies: Les Productions Lazennec, Le Studio Canal+, La Sept Cinéma

Pg. 129 — *Saving Private Ryan* (1998), starring: Tom Hanks, Matt Damon, Tom Sizemore / Writer: Robert Rodat / Director: Steven Spielberg / Production companies: Dreamworks Pictures, Paramount Pictures, Amblin Entertainment

Pg. 131 — *Get Out* (2017), Starring: Daniel Kaluuya, Allison Williams, Bradley Whitford / Writer: Jordan Peele / Director: Jordan Peele / Production companies: Universal Pictures, Blumhouse Productions, QC Entertainment

Pg. 133 — *12 Years a Slave* (2013), starring: Chiwetel Ejiofor, Michael Kenneth Williams, Michael Fassbender / Writers: John Ridley & Solomon Northup / Director: Steve McQueen / Production companies: New Regency Productions, River Road Entertainment, Plan B Entertainment

Pg. 135 — *Scarface* (1983), starring: Al Pacino, Michelle Pfeiffer, Steven Bauer / Writers: Oliver Stone, Howard Hawks, & Ben Hecht / Director: Brian De Palma / Production company: Universal Pictures

Pg. 137 — *Train to Busan* (2016), original title: *Busanhaeng* / Starring: Gong Yoo, Jung Yu-mi, Ma Dong-seok / Writers: Joo-Suk Park & Sang-ho Yeon / Director: Sang-ho Yeon / Production companies: Next Entertainment World (NEW), RedPeter Film, Movic Comics

Pg. 139 — *Scream* (1996), starring: Neve Campbell, Courteney Cox, David Arquette / Writer: Kevin Williamson / Director: Wes Craven / Production companies: Dimension Films, Woods Entertainment

Pg. 141 — *Predator* (1987), starring: Arnold Schwarzenegger, Carl Weathers, Kevin Peter Hall / Writers: Jim Thomas & John Thomas / Director: John McTiernan / Production companies: Twentieth Century Fox, Lawrence Gordon Productions, Silver Pictures

Pg. 143 — *The Fugitive* (1993), starring: Harrison Ford, Tommy Lee Jones, Sela Ward / Writers: Jeb Stuart, David Twohy, & Roy Huggins / Direeector: Andrew Davis / Production companies: Warner Bros., Kopelson Entertainment

Pg. 145 — *The Talented Mr Ripley* (1999), starring: Matt Damon, Gwyneth Paltrow, Jude Law / Writers: Patricia Highsmith & Anthony Minghella / Director: Anthony Minghella / Production companies: Miramax, Paramount Pictures, Mirage Enterprises

Pg. 147 — *The Silence of the Lambs* (1991), starring: Jodie Foster, Anthony Hopkins, Lawrence A. Bonney / Writers: Thomas Harris & Ted Tally / Director: Jonathan Demme / Production companies: Strong Heart/Demme Production, Orion Pictures

Pg. 149 — *The Exorcist* (1973), starring: Ellen Burstyn, Max von Sydow, Linda Blair / Writer: William Peter Blatty / Director: William Friedkin / Production companies: Warner Bros., Hoya Productions

Pg. 151 — Psycho (1960), starring: Anthony Perkins, Janet Leigh, Vera Miles / Writers: Joseph Stefano & Robert Bloch / Director: Alfred Hitchcock / Production company: Shamley Productions

Pg. 153 — *The Wicker Man* (1973), starring: Edward Woodward, Christopher Lee, Diane Cilento / Writers: Anthony Shaffer & David Pinner / Director: Robin Hardy / Production company: British Lion Film Corporation

Pg. 155 — *Gone Girl* (2014), starring: Ben Affleck, Rosamund Pike, Neil Patrick Harris / Writer: Gyllian Flynn / Director: David Fincher / Production companies: Twentieth Century Fox, New Regency Productions, TSG Entertainment

Pg. 157 — *It* (2017), starring: Bill Skarsgård, Jaeden Martell, Finn Wolfhard / Writers: Chase Palmer, Cary Joji Fukunaga, & Gary Dauberman / Director: Andy Muschietti / Production companies: New Line Cinema, RatPac-Dune Entertainment, Vertigo Entertainment

Pg. 159 – *Killing of a Sacred Deer* (2017), starring: Barry G. Bernson, Herb Caillouet, Bill Camp / Writers: Yorgos Lanthimos & Efthimis Filippou / Director: Yorgos Lanthimos / Production companies: Element Pictures, A24, Film4

Pg. 161 – *Indiana Jones and the Last Crusade* (1989) starring: Harrison Ford, Sean Connery, Alison Doody / Writers: Jeffrey Boam, George Lucas, & Menno Meyjes / Director: Steven Spielberg / Production companies: Paramount Pictures, Lucasfilm

Pg. 163 – *Jurassic Park* (1993), starring: Sam Neill, Laura Dern, Jeff Goldblum / Writers: Michael Crichton & David Koepp / Director: Steven Spielberg / Production companies: Universal Pictures, Amblin Entertainment

Pg. 165 – *Inception* (2010), starring: Leonardo DiCaprio, Joseph Gordon-Levitt, Elliot Page / Writer: Christopher Nolan / Director: Christopher Nolan / Production companies: Warner Bros., Legendary Entertainment, Syncopy

Pg. 167 – *Cast Away* (2000), starring: Tom Hanks, Helen Hunt, Paul Sanchez / Writer: William Broyles Jr. / Director: Robert Zemeckis / Production companies: Twentieth Century Fox, Dreamworks Pictures, ImageMovers

Pg. 169 – *The Wizard of Oz* (1939), starring: Judy Garland, Frank Morgan, Ray Bolger / Writers: Noel Langley, Florence Ryerson, & Edgar Allan Woolf / Directors: Victor Fleming, George Cukor, & Mervyn LeRoy / Production company: Metro-Goldwyn-Mayer (MGM)

Pg. 171 – *Life of Pi* (2012), starring: Suraj Sharma, Irrfan Khan, Adil Hussain / Writers: Yann Martel & David Magee / Director: Ang Lee / Production companies: Fox 2000 Pictures, Dune Entertainment, Ingenious Media

Pg. 173 – *Harry Potter and the Prisoner of Azkaban* (2004), Starring: Daniel Radcliffe, Emma Watson, Rupert Grint / Writers: J.K. Rowling & Steve Kloves / Director: Alfonso Cuarón / Production companies: Warner Bros.,1492 Pictures, Heyday Films

Pg. 175 – *The Borrowers* (1997), starring: John Goodman, Jim Broadbent, Mark Williams / Writers: Mary Norton, Gavin Scott, & John Kamps / Director: Peter Hewitt / Production companies: Polygram Filmed Entertainment, Working Title Films

Pg. 177 – *The Matrix* (1999), starring: Keanu Reeves, Laurence Fishburne, Carrie-Anne Moss / Writers: Lilly Wachowski & Lana Wachowski / Director: Lilly Wachowski & Lana Wachowski / Production companies: Warner Bros., Village Roadshow Pictures, Groucho Film Partnership

Pg. 179 – *Terminator 2: Judgement Day* (1991), starring: Arnold Schwarzenegger, Linda Hamilton, Edward Furlong / Writers: James Cameron & William Wisher / Director: James Cameron / Production companies: Carolco Pictures, Pacific Western, Lightstorm Entertainment

Pg. 181 – *Apollo 13* (1995), starring: Tom Hanks, Bill Paxton, Kevin Bacon / Writers: Jim Lovell, Jeffrey Kluger, & William Broyles Jr. / Director: Ron Howard / Production companies: Universal Pictures, Imagine Entertainment

Pg. 183 – *Underworld* (2003), starring: Kate Beckinsale, Scott Speedman, Shane Brolly / Writers: Kevin Grevioux, Len Wiseman, & Danny McBride / Director: Len Wiseman / Production companies: Lakeshore Entertainment, Screen Gems, Subterranean Productions UK Ltd.

Pg. 185 – *Honey, I Shrunk the Kids* (1989), starring: Rick Moranis, Matt Frewer, Marcia Strassman / Writers: Stuart Gordon, Brian Yuzna, & Ed Naha / Director: Joe Johnston / Production companies: Walt Disney Pictures, Silver Screen Partners III, Doric Productions

Pg. 187 – *Jungle Book* (1967), starring: Phil Harris, Sebastian Cabot, Louis Prima / Writers: Larry Clemmons, Ralph Wright, & Ken Anderson / Director: Wolfgang Reitherman / Production company: Walt Disney Animation Studios

Milton Keynes UK
Ingram Content Group UK Ltd.
UKHW020058071123
432073UK00001B/19